INSIDE

OUT

I0211398

This book is written for those who are in prison and out and to the men and women, the volunteers, who go to prison by choice.

I want to bring attention to the volunteers who travel each day at their own expense, leaving their families to spend time with incarcerated men and women for one purpose and one purpose only: to bring the saving grace and love of Jesus Christ into the lives of those who are behind bars. To visit the incarcerated is not an easy, convenient, or self-serving enterprise. There are times when they could have stayed on the couch and passed on the visit. But there is a calling within their lives that they cannot resist. See Alonzo's testimony, Chapter 7 or Casey Diaz Chapter 4, of how the visit of volunteers into a solitary confinement unit not only changed the life of the man they witnessed to, but has had a continuing influence on hundreds of men and women who were looking for a solution to their brokenness. The visits require dedication and real commitment to the God Work at hand. When you hear the sound of prison gates slamming behind you for the first time, one realizes that the banner of Christ needs to be planted within the walls. The volunteers are doing the planting and defending it with the Gospel.

INSIDE

OUT

Stories of Redemption From Prison

*A*dvantage
BOOKS

Kenneth C. McKenzie

INSIDE OUT by Kenneth C. McKenzie
Copyright © 2024 by Kenneth C. McKenzie
All Rights Reserved.
ISBN: 978-1-59755-813-6
Published by: ADVANTAGE BOOKS™
Saint Johns, FL USA
www.advbookstore.com

Unless otherwise noted, all scriptures are from the NEW AMERICAN STANDARD BIBLE®, Copyright© 1960, 1962, 1963, 1968, 1971, 1972, 1973, 1975, 1977, 1995 by The Lockman Foundation. Used by permission.

Scriptures marked NIV are taken from the NEW INTERNATIONAL VERSION®. Copyright© 1973, 1978, 1984, 2011 by Biblica, Inc.TM. Used by permission of Zondervan.

Scriptures marked BSB are taken from the Berean Standard Bible which is public domain.

Library of Congress Catalog Number: 2024951326	
Names:	McKenzie, Kenneth C.
Title:	*INSIDE OUT: Stories of Redemption From Prison*
	Kenneth C. McKenzie, Author
	Advantage Books, 2024
Identifiers:	ISBN Paperback: 9781597558136
	ISBN eBook: 9781597558242
Subjects:	Christian Life - Inspirational
	Christian Life – Faith
	Christian Life – Self Help

Published December 2024
25 26 27 28 29 30 31 10 9 8 7 6 5 4 3 2 1

TESTIMONIALS

Having lived the majority of my adult life in the company of inmates as a prison warden, I know too well the stories of the men and women whose names have been reduced to a number. Yet, while prisons are some of the darkest places on earth, many of those who "did their time" are released only to return again, and again. The life stories that make up this book, written directly from the spoken words of the former prisoners themselves, leads the reader to discover what they each have in common that brought them to the point of living their lives outside of prison bars. Thank you Ken for your vision and tenacity in sharing their stories and using them as an inspiration, "If God can do that for "these" people think then what He can do for me".

Jack Cowley, National Director, Damascus Reentry Inc. Division of Institutions

****

A person's testimony of what God has done in their life holds incredible power to influence and transform others. Each story is a unique reflection of grace, redemption, and hope, serving as a tangible reminder of God's presence and faithfulness. When individuals share their experiences, they not only illuminate the path of faith for others but also inspire them to believe in the possibility of change and healing. Ultimately, these stories will create a ripple effect—encouraging others to explore their own faith journeys and seek the transformative love that can only come from a personal encounter with the Jesus.

Bruce Paulus, National Deputy Director, Damascus Reentry Inc. Division of Institutions,

****

Ken McKenzie has facilitated the compilation of powerful and uplifting stories of redemption – testimonials - from men and women whose lives of desperation were changed forever by discovering the love of God. The discovery process often involves someone who chooses to believe in the potential of a "thug" and lends a helping hand, demonstrating the importance of forgiveness and second chances. Ultimately, the discovery of Jesus and the love of God has a multiplier effect as reformed thugs are now sharing their compelling stories with others.

Warren Blanchard

****

Do not be deceived: neither the sexually immoral, nor idolaters, nor adulterers, nor men who practice homosexuality, nor thieves, nor the greedy, nor drunkards, nor revilers, nor swindlers will inherit the kingdom of God. **And such were some of you**. But you were washed, you were sanctified, you were justified in the name of the Lord Jesus Christ and by the Spirit of our God."This verse serves as a reminder of the transformative power of God's grace, where people who have lived in sin can be forgiven and made new through faith in Jesus. Through the experiences of these men and women serving hard time for committing a lengthy list of heinous crimes against God (Genesis 39:9), the redemptive story of the ages unfolds in alarming detail in their lives. We are left to shake our heads in total wonderment at the perseverance, patience, and purposes of God being worked out in space and time through shocking circumstances. Like Jonah, all ran from God in their own way. And like Jonah, God in His way brought them home to Himself for His Glory, their good, and the spread of His Kingdom.

Richard R. Glau, Th.M , Manager, Faith Based Services, The GEO Group, INC.

****

There is no greater testimony of the power of the gospel than a changed life. Jesus Christ came and died for the sins of every human being who will ever live and has redeemed us literally from the pit of hell. " Inside Out - Stories of Redemption," is an incredibly emotional testimony of the power of the gospel to change lives. The stories of redemption of seemingly unredeemable people caught in Satan's grip should be an encouragement to every believer in Jesus. I highly recommend the book, but especially for those who think that God can't enable them to snatch victory from the jaws of defeat. It reminds me of the beginning of Psalm 40, a Psalm of David -

I waited patiently for the LORD;
And He inclined to me and heard my cry.
He brought me up out of the pit of destruction, out of the miry clay,
And He set my feet upon a rock making my footsteps firm.
He put a new song in my mouth, a song of praise to our God;

Dr. Richard Freeman, Vice President of Chosen People Ministries

****

Ken McKenzie is passionate about changing the lives of people who have been left behind. This book will inspire and challenge you to believe that there is no one beyond God's reach, which is why we need to keep taking the gospel of Jesus to every person in every place on earth.

Pastor Jimmy Scroggins, Lead Pastor, Family Church, Florida

****

The stories you hold in your hand are a powerful testimony of the Amazing Grace of Jesus Christ. He is a God who loves to work in the most unlikely places, and through the most unlikely people. Read this book and let your own faith be encouraged through the stories of these men and women. God not only wants to continue working in the prisons, He wants to work in and through YOU too!

Joel McDonald, Pastor, Family Church West, Florida

****

Ken has put together an excellent account of ruined lives rescued by Christ. The accounts are a dark and disturbing record of broken and destroyed souls through sin. In every case, their lives have been forever changed by the miracle of Christ's salvation. Darkness becomes Light. Despair becomes Hope. Jesus Christ makes all things new. The life-changing work of Christ, as depicted in this book demonstrates the hope of mankind in Christ. If your life seems lost, hopeless, destroyed by sin, come read what Christ has done in the healing of the souls of these men and women. He can heal you too if you put your trust in Him! What has begun in this life for these souls who have found Christ is only the beginning of what is to come. The best is yet to be!

"Revelation 21:5 And he that sat upon the throne said, Behold, I make all things new. And he said unto me, Write: for these words are true and faithful." What a Great Savior we have!

Pastor Henry Stankey

****

God changes things. I know that is true, but I never knew it the way these men and women do.

These stories shredded my shallow ideas of how much prisoners must overcome from their past abuse and poor choices outside. With stunning casualness, they describe how awful and violent, how hopeless and depressing their lives were inside. But God met them right where they were. The Lord Jesus comes to them through people who love them before they are lovable. Soaking in Biblical truth opens their minds and softens their hearts, and they are changed! These stories fill me with hope because our Lord has called us to care for the prisoner. May our Lord's love continue to kindle revival fires among prisoners who are surely among the least of these to whom Christ has called us. Thank you, Ken, for these stories of miraculous redemption and hope.

Gary Ginter

****

Discover the life-changing stories in *Inside Out - Stories of Redemption* by Ken McKenzie, where men and women once lost in darkness find hope and renewal behind prison walls. These real-life accounts, drawn from the acclaimed *Death Or Prison* podcast, reveal how even the most broken lives can be transformed through faith in Jesus Christ. Raw, inspiring, and filled with unexpected grace, this book offers a message of hope for anyone seeking proof of redemption.

Pastor Christian Ramos

****

A compelling read that takes you on an emotional journey through the lives of those seeking redemption. These stories are raw, honest, and filled with hope, illustrating that even in the most challenging circumstances, true transformation is possible through the saving grace of our Lord and Savior.

Paul Allen, Military Veteran and Special Agent, FBI.

****

It is in your hands to create a better world for all who live in it." Nelson Mandela. This quote emphasizes the importance of taking responsibility for one's actions and making the world a better place through our efforts, which is the foundation of rehabilitation and reintegration in community corrections. Mandela's words serve as a reminder that both individuals under supervision and the systems supporting them have the power to effect positive change.

Joe Winkler, Assistant Secretary Community Corrections, Florida Department of Corrections.

****

Do not be deceived: neither the sexually immoral, nor idolaters, nor adulterers, nor men who practice homosexuality, nor thieves, nor the greedy, nor drunkards, nor revilers, nor swindlers will inherit the kingdom of God. **And such were some of you**. But you were washed, you were sanctified, you were justified in the name of the Lord Jesus Christ and by the Spirit of our God." This verse serves as a reminder of the transformative power of God's grace, where people who have lived in sin can be forgiven and made new through faith in Jesus. Through the experiences of these men and women serving hard time for committing a lengthy list of heinous crimes against God (Genesis 39:9), the redemptive story of the ages unfolds in alarming detail in their lives. We are left to shake our heads in total wonderment at the perseverance, patience, and purposes of God being worked out in space and time through shocking circumstances. Like Jonah, all ran from God in their own way. And like Jonah, God in His way brought them home to Himself for His Glory, their good, and the spread of His Kingdom.

Richard R. Glau, Th.M , Manager, Faith Based Services, The GEO Group, INC.

****

Table of Contents

Kenneth C. McKenzie

INTRODUCTION

"Through the cell bars and prison walls He came and entered their hearts." Kenneth C. McKenzie

I was a Special Agent for the FBI beginning in 1968 and worked in the Washington Field Office, Philadelphia and Los Angeles offices on bank robbery, fugitive and surveillance squads. I assisted on Top Ten arrests and still hold the record for being the case Agent for the largest bank robbery crew ever arrested in Los Angeles, eleven in all.

I had come home from Vietnam in 1967 with a bullet near my spine, having been shot with an AK47 from about thirty feet away. At the time I didn't know why I was so lucky and had been saved but what I came to realize is that luck is just another nickname for God. Never did I expect to be given the privilege to share the stories of redemption so passionately told by the men and women who are the chapters in this book. Nor did I realize that I might one day influence others to look for God's plan in their lives. As we live our lives too often from the inside, we must never forget that God's plan for our outside is service to others.

In 2020, I had produced three episodes of a podcast designed to bring hope, encouragement, inspiration, but more importantly God Almighty into prisons worldwide, but I was still searching for the podcast's name, one that would be a gabber. Before the fourth filming, a guest told me, "There are only two ways out of the 'hood; death or prison." That was it, I didn't need to search further. Those words were a powerful punch that made me realize, "No, wrong, there is a third way; the Lord God Almighty and His son Jesus." Death Or Prison became the new title for the podcast and the prison walls could not keep the Glory of God out!

Jesus Christ in the Bible tells believers to take the Gospel to the world, to all the nations. The United States locks up more people per capita than any other nation on earth. Presently, there are approximately 2,000,000 confined in the United States alone. To my mind, those men and women constitute a nation, one of those that Jesus commissioned us to go to. Presently the podcast is available on approximately 1,500,000 electronic tablets distributed in prisons nationwide, GloryStar Satellite Television, a global Christian outreach network, and ROKU TV, The "LIT" channel.

My inspiration for writing this book are the men and women whose lives "happen" within the pages. They are extraordinary people. All have appeared on the Death Or Prison podcast and have given their remarkable, inspiring testimonies of restoration before the camera. Good portions of their lives have been lived behind bars for crimes they committed in an earlier life. Some of the crimes were heinous. Murder, drugs, armed robberies and desperation were once what their lives were driven by and revolved around. They were different people then, living dark lives and in society's eyes, unlikely candidates to be saved.

Their stories are in many cases overwhelmingly sad until they get to the point in which they detail how their thinking changed and redemption happened the moment they invited Jesus Christ into their lives. There is nothing like discovering that God loves you, and is with you when you are in prison full of despair. Surprisingly, many during the interviews confessed that they are grateful for being locked up because as they saw it, incarceration was the only way they would have found salvation.

The men and women are not bitter at the system, they are not angry, they carry no hatred, they are not filled with animosity. Rather, they are filled with gratitude for the second chance they received. More often than not many confessed, prior to their change the real prison was the prison of their minds. They have escaped that prison and definitively, today they are different, restored people. Some are now Pastors leading their flocks away from the crimes they committed. Some could be Pastors. But all are dedicated to serving the God who took them out of their life behind the physical and mental bars and gave them freedom through their belief in Jesus Christ.

These stories have been taken directly from interviews before a camera and transcribed onto paper. Some editorial discretion has taken place, words have been rearranged, deleted and/or added. Each guest has been provided the opportunity to make changes to the transcript as they wished. I wanted the stories to be theirs, not mine, all to the glory of God.

The stories could not have happened were it not for the volunteering spirit and dedication to the effort of the emcees of the podcast, my family of men, Elmo Golden, Johnny Branham, Raul Lopez, Laz Lopez, Oswald Newbold and Kevin Sabbath. In total, these six men have 98 years of prison and jail time between them. They all were once thugs but now they are hugs, thanks be to God.

I hope you will open your heart and mind to explore your own faith as you travel through these testimonies of redemption and in your daily life continue to do The God Work.

100% of all monies received from the sale of this book will go to the 501 (c)(3) charity, Lean On Me USA.org, producer of the Death Or Prison podcast.

Kenneth C. McKenzie, CEO, Lean On Me USA, Producer, Death Or Prison Podcast

Kenneth C. McKenzie

1

"A Twice Decorated Soldier
A Red Cadillac
and
The Death Penalty"

"I know that the experiences of our lives, when we let God use them, become the mysterious preparation for the work He will give us to do."

Corrie Ten Boom, *"The Hiding Place."*

42 years locked inside prison walls. Try to imagine that. Ricky and I have become friends, talking on the phone after his interviews on the Death Or Prison Podcast took place and always either starting or ending the conversation with, "Airborne!" and the response, "All the way!" That is exactly how far Ricky has come - all the way.

HOLLAND RICKY WHITE
Death Or Prison podcast, Numbers 67 and 68
42 years inside.

I grew up in a very turbulent, crime infested neighborhood in Fort Lauderdale, Broward County, Florida, in the 1950's. I attended Dillard Elementary and Dillard High School. In my neighborhood, ladies of the night, pimps, hustlers, drugs, alcoholism were common and made up the lifestyle of our community. I was living in the midst of that environment and it had an impact upon my life, upon my growth and thinking as a child. In addition and making the situation worse, Jim Crow laws were in effect and segregation was forced upon the black community.

Being black, I felt restricted, unable to do certain things. I felt I wasn't a human being. I felt out of place. I didn't have an answer to what was going on in my life, I only had questions. A lot of turmoil, a lot of resentment, a lot of anger, a lot of hate filled me. I was instructed by my dad that whenever I went downtown and I encountered someone of a different color, I was to bow my head, keep it down and lower my eyes and in a sense, humiliate myself. I was to be submissive. As a boy between the ages of 11 or 12, I couldn't understand that rule. I thought it was very degrading. These were very, very difficult times. So I rebelled.

Strangely enough, I didn't experience any violence when I was downtown. But in the neighborhood where I lived that was a different story. There was a lot of violence and I learned how to protect myself, how to survive. We had gangs yes, but gangs then weren't the same as they are today. We were territorial. We took care of a particular area, our area, our neighborhood. I created a name for myself and I became a part of the gang environment and thinking that went along with it. I was a very bitter, and very, very angry young man.

Most of the time I was mad at myself in a sense, because of where I was living. Fifth Avenue was the heart of the black ghetto community in Broward County. It was infested with crime and I was living in the middle of it. When I had to go to school and be around some of my classmates who lived in a different, better area of town, that disparity got to me also. So what were my expectations? I didn't have any good ones.

Then one day in 1967 I got home from school and looked in the mailbox. There was a letter addressed to me from the President of the United States telling me that I had been inducted, drafted into the armed forces. 1967 was the height of the Vietnam war.

I said to myself, "Well, I'm either going to the Army or I'm going to the Marines. I'm going somewhere." First, I immediately went to a Marine recruiter because I had it in my mind that I wanted to be a Marine if I had to fight for this country. The recruiter told me they weren't accepting anyone who hadn't finished high school.

Yes, I was still in high school. So I went to the Army recruiter and I showed him the letter. He said, "We're good," meaning I could join. I was sent to Fort Benning, Georgia, where I did my basic infantry training. After I completed basic, I volunteered for Airborne School which was three weeks long and five parachute jumps at the end. I was 'Airborne' and proud. Immediately, I was transferred from Airborne training to Fort Sill, Oklahoma, to take artillery training. I finished artillery training and I was then sent to Fort Lee, Virginia, for parachute rigger school. I learned how to pack parachutes.

After that training, orders came down sending me to the Republic of Vietnam. How did I feel as a black man going to fight for this country? I felt compelled to go because we were fighting for a cause to curtail Communism and to keep it from spreading from North Vietnam to South Vietnam. This is what we were told. I was a soldier, it was my duty and responsibility to honor those orders.

Was I conflicted? I realized that my training in the military got me out of the hood. I was given the opportunity to put a weapon in my hand legally and the license to take a life. This was what my country asked me to do and I didn't have a problem. I felt relieved to leave the environment I grew up in, to go to a different place and see other parts of the world. I felt it important to go and perform the duty and the task I was given. So I got sent to Vietnam. I felt this was alright. "Maybe," I told myself, "I can find out who I really am."

I did three tours in Vietnam beginning January, 1968. I returned to the States in January, 1970, a highly decorated soldier with two Bronze Stars, both with V Device for Valor.

I remember the first Bronze Star I received. My unit was on top of a hill called Corregidor in the A Shau valley where there were some big battles in the months leading up to this time. We had six 105 millimeter howitzer guns on top of that hill. We were being overrun one night and what I mean by overrun, we had the 3rd NVA Regiment coming to take that hill, kill us and capture those guns. The howitzers were very central and important to the Viet Cong, "Charley," because they knew if they had those artillery pieces, they could create a lot of havoc by turning them around and using them against our troops.

Charley had a way of overrunning a hill position. He had sappers and they carried explosive charges, homemade devices filled with glass, nails, explosives and when they went off the stuff went in all directions. The explosion could kill or maim you real quick. They also had mortars and 122-millimeter rockets. They hit us very hard that night. It was a desperate battle. They were trying to get through our perimeter wire and when the incoming started we knew they were coming after us hard, it was us or them, so we knew immediately we had to do our thing to stay alive.

During the fight, a satchel charge hit the parapet of my gun section and it blew me back into my hooch, my sleeping place that I had dug deep into the ground. After I regained consciousness, I immediately got my M16, climbed on one of the 105 mm howitzers and started firing the big gun with what we called MTS2 fuzes, multiple time, super quick fuzes. I was shooting at the wire. We also had what we called a Beehive round made of small pieces of metal shards that when fired would scatter and I fired those rounds at the perimeter wire and at the men trying to get through.

In gun section 3, a brother who was part of my unit, was fighting and a 122 rocket came in and...it just took him, it obliterated him. The only thing left of him was a shoe. I stood up and just started shooting my M16 at the perimeter. It was a long night.

When the sun came up, I saw many enemy bodies on the barbed wire. They were everywhere. The commanding general came out that morning in a helicopter and awarded me the Bronze Star with V Device for Valor. This is not something I like to talk about. It was a very traumatic experience because the guy who was obliterated was a very good and close friend. In the military, you have comrades at arms, brothers you befriend and assist. He was a good buddy but he was no longer around.

The entire experience that night gave me a new way of thinking about myself. I got a sense of being someone as opposed to thinking I wasn't anyone. When I returned to the States in January 1970, the Army stationed me at Fort Bragg, North Carolina, with the 82 Airborne Division as a Staff Sergeant E6 assigned to Division Artillery. I was placed in a unit and given the responsibility of training new recruits. I was like a Drill Sergeant. I excelled at PT, Physical Training. We ran five miles every morning and we did calisthenics. We exercised with what we called the Daily Dozen.

I was training a new recruit in my unit who was a private. He had been through Basic and Advanced Training. We were doing PT one morning and he was kind of slack. So I asked him, "Private, what's wrong with you? You have a problem doing PT?" He said, "I'm not going to listen to anything you say." And he called me the "N" word.

I just blew, I lost it. Everything that happened to me in the '60s came back to me, the Jim Crow era and how I had to conduct myself. I physically assaulted him and as a result I was held for Court Martial. The Presiding Officer was my Battalion Commander who was also my Battalion Commander in Vietnam. He had awarded me my stripes and had recommended that I receive my first Bronze Star.

After the trial, I got busted down in rank to a Buck Sergeant, Sergeant E5. I lost a Stripe and the Army charged me $135 for two months. After that proceeding, I had no desire to stay in the United States military. I had gone to Vietnam, I had fought for and served my country and then when I came back home I wasn't welcome, I was insulted. All of us who came home from Vietnam were called every name you could think of including degenerates and baby killers. And on top of that, I got called the "N" word. I was bitter because I had served honorably and had done what my country required of me. I had lost comrades at arms in Vietnam and for me to be considered just another N, that was very offensive to me. So I got out. Because of my Vietnam record I accumulated over the time that I was in service, I was given an Honorable Discharge.

Leaving the Army I went from Fort Bragg to Fort Lauderdale. I went to the Florida State Employment Office and got a job as an employment counselor. I had an opportunity to meet a lot of people who were on unemployment and the majority were female. The job wasn't fulfilling, it was a source of income. I kept it for awhile but I had some friends who were involved in selling drugs and they kept asking me, "Hey Ricky, why are you working for the Employment Office when you can make more money selling drugs?" I had used drugs when I was in Vietnam. I had smoked Marijuana and drank a lot of alcohol. Virtually everybody smoked and drank when we came back into base camp from the field so drugs were no stranger to me.

When I came home, I drank alcohol very heavily and I used a variety of drugs. I experimented with barbiturates, amphetamine and black beauties. I didn't realize at that time that I was addicted but later on the addiction took its toll and had an effect on me. Addiction can lead us to do things, crazy things. I was what you would call a Sophisticated Junkie.

I remembered a time when I was young and impressionable, a guy named Johnny from the hood where I grew up and he had a red Cadillac. I'll never forget that convertible Cadillac. He had three beautiful young ladies step out of that Cadillac one day. As a kid seeing these three lovely ladies and that red Cadillac, wow, I wondered if some day I could have that. So I set out to make it happen. I got into being what the streets called a street pimp. I got girls to work for me, I took on the life and sold drugs as well. In the 1970's there was a lot of movin 'and groovin 'and I started meeting people, musical people, influential people.

One year there was a national pimp's convention at the Fontainebleau in Miami which I took the girls to. I had the big hat with the fur jacket, the MaxiCoat, tailor made clothes, the Fly Collar and at the hotel I stepped out of a 'Hog,' a big Cadillac. I had a salt and pepper team with me; on my right sleeve was a black female and on my left sleeve was a white female.

Chaka Khan was playing at the hotel and nobody could tell me I wasn't doin 'my thing. The girls were working, I was snorting cocaine, smoking marijuana and drinking alcohol with the money I made. I had progressed with using drugs to where there were only going to be two future outcomes for me; the graveyard or the jail, death or prison like the name says.

I was selling cocaine and pharmaceutical pills, Dilauded and Black Beauties. I fixed my girls up with Doctors who gave them exams to make sure they were clean of all diseases. The Doctors would write prescriptions for drugs, any and all that I needed. The Beauties were Amphetamine. The Doctors wrote scripts for 20, 30, 40 Dilauded at a time. I filled the scripts and sold the pills for $20 each and I was selling a lot of them. I had a particular pharmacy that I frequented where I filled the prescriptions.

I went to this pharmacy soon after the convention and something terrible happened, something went horribly wrong, an accident occurred and I took the life of the Pharmacist. I left the place where it all went down and eluded law enforcement for a period of months. I was finally apprehended one morning after collecting drug money from one of my sellers. I got the money and drove to a gas station next door to get some gas. All of a sudden three carloads of officers surrounded me with weapons drawn and all yelling, "If you move we will shoot." I didn't move and asked, "What's the charge?" They said they had an outstanding bench warrant for a traffic violation but the charge they put on me when I was booked was First Degree Murder. They took me to the Broward County jail and I was locked up.

I will never forget that place because when I was put in there I heard the sound of steel banging against steel. And the thought came to my mind, "I am going to be in here a very long time." Before that, I didn't think I was ever going to get caught, it had never crossed my mind. However, I did get caught and I was facing the death penalty.

My case was highly publicized along with another one out of Miami, the "television intoxicated" killer Ronnie Zamora. They had television coverage inside both our courtrooms and those trials were the first trials ever to be televised in the State of Florida. My prosecutor asked for the death penalty. I had a 12 person empaneled jury. I had a paid defense attorney and I was prosecuted by the State Prosecutor himself along with the Chief Homicide Prosecutor.

I went to trial and it lasted 14 days. I was found guilty of premeditated murder. However, in a capital murder case, there is a section of the law that says the jury can make a recommendation to the Judge whether or not to give life in prison or death. Thinking of this, my attorney told me that we needed to introduce to the jury my combat record, my Vietnam service record, the fact that I had served this country honorably and that I had received decorations from the military for my service.

My attorney introduced my combat record as a mitigating circumstance. The jury came back and found me guilty of premeditated first degree murder but recommended that I do life in prison instead of getting the death penalty, the Florida electric chair. The Judge took their recommendation, waived the death penalty and sentenced me to life in prison. I was 28 years old, still a young man and now I was headed to the 'steel on steel' sound I remembered from the county jail for what I thought was the rest of my life.

When the trial ended, I was flown to Lake Butler Correctional Institution in a small Piper airplane. Because of my Vietnam record the authorities didn't want to take the chance that I might try to escape. Lake Butler had an airstrip and when I landed, two people met me, Lieutenant Young, aka "N" Charley, yes, the N word, and K. Wayne Slim. They told me they had 'been waiting on me.' They took me directly to K Wing. They placed me on K Wing and said, "You are going to the East Unit." I asked, "What is the East Unit?" They told me I would find out when I got there.

I didn't end up in the East Unit but I ended up right across the street at a place they call 'The Rock,' Union Correctional Institution, UCI, better known as Raiford CI. There were three thousand inmates there in three separate areas, the Southwest Unit, The Rock and the West Unit. My mindset was to survive, to utilize everything I had learned in my life both from the streets as a youth and as a combat veteran. I knew Raiford, The Rock, was notorious for being excessively violent. It ranked with Sing Sing and San Quentin in California for being a tough place. It was up there with the hardest of the hard. I figured I had to use what I learned in Vietnam in order to survive such an adverse, dangerous environment.

When I got there I was very bitter, bitter at the State of Florida because this was my first offense. Yes my crime was murder, but I had no criminal record, no previous conviction and I received a mandatory 25 year life sentence. I saw other guys with similar crimes and similar charges receiving just life in prison. And at that time, a life sentence meant doing 12 and a half years and if you could make good time, you could get out. But I was given a different, stiffer sentence and I was very, very angry and bitter. It was rough.

In 1978, 60 Minutes came and did an interview with the Raiford Staff. They were doing a story of a survey that had been conducted of the killing rates at various prisons. The survey indicated that Raiford was the fiercest prison in the United States. An inmate was dying, getting killed every month. I knew all of this and the truth made me even more determined to survive. I started selling drugs and marijuana on the compound and I gained a little influence. Guys knew that I sold marijuana and would come to me for a sale.

I'll never forget that in 1980 I went to the movie 'Superman 'in the main housing unit. I had just received a pound of weed and I took an ounce with me, rolled it into a blunt and I was smoking it, watching the movie when all of a sudden I felt something in my side, a knife. I looked at the guy and said, "Are you crazy? Do you know who I am?"

He said, "I don't care who you are," and the next thing I know, I feel an arm going around my neck and I'm being choked out.

I was out for a few minutes. The lights came on, Officers asked me if I was alright and I told them I was fine. But they took me to the OPC, the Out Patient Clinic, the hospital at Raiford. En-route, a guy asked me, "Ricky, you know who did that to you?" I said no and he gave me the two guy's names. So I went to the OPC and after release I waited two weeks. I picked my time and went back to the movies with a plan.

When I returned to movie night, I was strapped down and ready. I had two knives. I wrapped myself up with knee bands all the way around my body to protect me. I had my jacket on and I went looking for the guys. During the movie, I saw one make a move down a short pathway that led to the bathroom and I saw him go inside. I followed him in.

Before all this went down, my homeboy said, "Ricky, you're a convicted murderer. If you kill this guy, you're going to get the electric chair." He gave me a pipe. I guess he figured a pipe was less lethal. I tied it around my hand. So I go up to this guy in the bathroom and I said, "Hey, you tried to rob me!" I hit him with the pipe on the side of his head. Once I hit him, I felt a stab in my back and I turned around to see his partner, the guy who had just stabbed me. I swung the pipe, and hit him. I was turning around to hit the first guy again but he had pulled a shank out of his sock and he stuck me in the neck. He got me good.

They rushed me to the OPC again. The nurse on duty wrapped my neck and tried to stop the bleeding but I was bleeding profusely. They couldn't do much to stop the flow. She called for the wagon, the ambulance, to take me to the hospital at Lake Butler. There was a Doctor there, a very nice Vietnamese Doctor. He told me he needed to take some X Rays. However, unknown to me, the ambulance driver was also my Classification Officer working part time because he needed to make some extra money. He told the Doctor that if he didn't get me to Shands Teaching Hospital, I was going to die. So the Officer rushed me via the ambulance to the Shands Hospital in Gainesville, Florida. He saved my life. The Professors and Doctors were waiting for me.

When I arrived they rushed me to surgery immediately. During the surgery, I died three times on the table. I didn't know this until I came out of surgery, was in intensive care and a lady Doctor came in and told me all about what had happened.

While I was healing, anger drove me to get better. Nothing reasonable resonated with me, I didn't change my thinking at all. I stayed hateful of this country and mad at my condition. I kept thinking of the sacrifices I had made. The thoughts kept going through my mind, driving me.

But it was God who had afforded me an opportunity to live and I didn't recognize that reality. Survival was still my only motive, God wasn't yet part of my life. I felt having a strong mindset together with my skills and talents would keep me alive. I had to depend on me, no one else, that's what I felt. I had no idea that God had His hand on me and was moving me forward for a purpose.

After the stabbing in 1981, I was transferred to Avon Park where I continued to recuperate. I was there for 4 years. In 1985 I was sent back to Raiford. I left Raiford after a year, then was sent to Baker CI, then to Belle Glade CI, Martin CI, then to DeSoto CI in 1987, to the main unit, then eventually to the annex. They moved me around a lot. I was involved in the law library everywhere I went and was filing grievances against the Florida Department of Corrections for living conditions and medical treatment of inmates. I was winning many disciplinary hearings for the guys. I had many DR's or Disciplinary Reports for the guys tossed out. I don't think the State liked or appreciated what I was doing. Besides all that, I was still selling dope and making wine.

It was in DeSoto CI in 1987, that I received a letter from the Secretary of the Florida Department of Corrections, Harry K. Singletary. The Secretary and I had been corresponding because of my many court filings. He told me in the letter that positive consideration for parole would not be forthcoming based upon my disciplinary record. I had a bad one. He was giving me advice. He told me that I needed to concentrate on adhering to the rules, minding my own business and to focus on getting out and staying out of prison. I still have that letter.

I didn't change much, I didn't take his advice. I stayed in the same mentality for another six years. Then in 1993, two things happened that had a big impact on me. The first was that I lost two brothers to AIDS during a span of one year and I started blaming God. I was on the yard one day and I angrily asked God, "Why are you punishing my family for the deeds I have done?" I told God to punish me if He wished to punish someone. Punish me and not my family, I told Him. Those were my two younger brothers. And it was then that I made my decision. It was a turning point in my life.

I told God, "No, this has gone too far!" and I got down on my hands and knees and cried like a baby. The floodgates opened up and I said, "Lord, I'm tired." I surrendered, I completely surrendered. I said to the Lord, "If you allow me an opportunity, I will serve you for the remaining years of my life."

I made that my vow to God in 1993 and told Him that I give it all to Him, that this was what I was going to do: I am going to get out and serve you God and to give back what you God, so freely gave to me.

Once you make a vow to God, you cannot break that vow. As of today, sitting here telling my story, I haven't broken that vow and I will not break that vow. I was sentenced to life and the only reason I am out and sitting here telling this story is that God's hand was upon me. I am a miracle. The State didn't change my sentence, God did.

The second thing that happened about the same time was that more than a decade after I got shanked in the neck and died three times on the table, I realized it was God who kept me alive all that time. It took me that long to realize it. Once I had that revelation a dramatic change occurred. I understood then that my life wasn't determined by me. It wasn't happening because of me, me, me, that my life was in God's hands. God afforded me an opportunity to live and to learn how to grow in His wisdom, His knowledge and in the understanding that He had given me. Before that revelation, I had never recognized any of this. He had never stopped carrying me all that time. He had had a plan for me.

Then I got moved to Polk CI around 2001. I still remember the morning of 9/11. I was repairing a television set and saw it happen. I didn't know it was real, I thought it was a commercial. At Polk at that time, there was an Administrator named Archie McDaniel. For some reason, Archie saw something in me I didn't see in myself. He saw potential, he told me I was a leader and that I was a guy who could do many things if I only utilized the skills that God had given me. I thought and thought about that. As a result I decided to continue my education.

I got transferred from Polk Correctional where Archie was, to Everglades CI in 2006. There, I got involved in Bible studies. I had an opportunity to attend a Bible college through a correspondence course. I earned my Bachelor Degree in Biblical Studies. I also started participating in other, different programs. That's why and how I got involved in the AVP, program, the Alternative to Violence Program. By this time I had made a complete change in my life, my education, my outlook, my thought patterns, everything. I had been inside for close to 30 years. It took me that long to realize what God wanted for my life.

God then told me, "Ricky, I'm going to allow you to run. But this is what I want you to do. Once you are out, I want you to go back inside and give your testimony to those guys in there. Let them know that despite everything that has happened to you, I let you out of prison, man did not release you. Go back in there and let those guys know that there is hope. Inspire them and let them know if they believe in Me, then everything is possible." And that is what I have been doing ever since the gates were opened and I paroled from Martin CI, a level 7 camp in August, 2019. I'll never forget it. I walked out after 42 years.

I have been out four and a half years and this is what God has accomplished in my life. Not Ricky, God. I carry two cards with me at all times; one is a card they give every inmate when he is checked in. I served

42 calendar years behind those fences with this card. The other is the Florida Department of Corrections Volunteer card. I can go into any prison conveying the message that there is life after prison if only you have hope, keep the faith and believe in the Lord and Savior Jesus Christ. He will open those doors. I am a living testimony to that fact.

After I was released, I accepted God's assignment. I am living my vow. I am now the Coordinator and Director of the Alternative to Violence Program in West Central Florida. I have implemented this Program in four institutions in region 3 of the Florida Department of Corrections. I have been back in six institutions in which I was housed and I have spoken to the men. I am co-sponsor of the Lifer Program and Gavel Club. I am also co-sponsor of Avon Park Veteran's Group. My experience taught me to let the men know that there is life after prison. My message is that Jesus opened the door to a new life for me. Guess what; He can do it for you.

I don't want this generation to end up like me spending precious, good years behind those fences. I tell the guys when I go back inside that the behavior we exhibited in an earlier life is not indicative of the life we can live now or of the behavior we should be exemplifying now. This is especially true after we accept Jesus Christ as Lord and Savior.

My ministry is predicated on love not anger. And that is the message I convey, one of changing thinking, especially stinking thinking. I say think about the people who care so much for you, about the people you have affected because of your actions. I say give it to God and He will be there for you.

Ricky is currently employed by the Jack Brewer Foundation as Program Facilitator for the Hero's Second Chance Fatherhood Initiative. He visits Florida prisons on an almost daily basis keeping his vow to God while telling his redemption story. Airborne All The Way!

2

"Molestation, Madness and Murder"

"If it's one thing we all know, life can be difficult." Life Insurance Advertisement

Marianne Van Dongen is a remarkable person in that she bears no anger, hostility or animosity for the sometimes cruel life she led as a child. Marianne's pre-teen and young adult years were filled with molestation and pain. The pain got worse as she moved forward in time. Today, however, her heart is filled with forgiveness and joy. She is living her rebirth into a new life filled with Jesus Christ.

MARIANNE VAN DONGEN
Death Or Prison podcast, Numbers 86 and 87
27 years inside.

I was born in the Naval Hospital in Augusta, Georgia, in 1966. My dad was in the Navy and was stationed in Georgia. After the birth of my younger brother and sister, we all moved to Mobile, Alabama.

After the move, my mom became mentally ill, unstable. I was about five at the time. There was a lot of abuse going on for my siblings and me. One time, my dad was overseas on assignment and my little brother was learning to walk. Mom didn't want him to walk because she didn't want to run after him. So she laid him across her lap, grabbed his legs, took a cigarette and burned the bottom of his feet so that he couldn't walk and she wouldn't have to chase him around.

On another occasion, my little brother and I were playing and he stabbed me in the eye with a pair of little blue scissors. My mom grabbed me and threw me into the car. I was crying and screaming and she was mad at me for making noise and she slapped me. The scissors went flying out of my eye. After the hospital took care of me, I remember wearing an eye-patch for almost six months.

When my dad returned home from his overseas tour and saw me he decided that mom was a hazard and that she would seriously harm us if he didn't take steps to get us away from her. He thought she might end up killing us. He didn't know what she would do next so he took us away from her.

My grandparents then came into the picture and helped my dad. They helped raise the three of us. They were the best. My mom was Baker Acted into a mental institution after we left her.

She had a complete mental breakdown. My dad then divorced my mom and left the military. Shortly after the divorce and leaving the Navy, he met my stepmother Lila, in a bar in Mobile, Alabama, where she worked as a bartender. He married Lila shortly after they met. They were both alcoholics.

After the marriage, we moved to Semmes, Alabama, in 1971. Lila had six boys, all older than me. I think the closest boy in age was seven years older. It was a trying situation, very challenging for me to be in a household suddenly with so many people.

Not all of us lived together in the house at the same time because there was a lot of coming and going. A lot of her sons, my brothers, were already grown, out of the house and they had girlfriends with kids.

We had some fun family get togethers, family reunions, barbecues and Sunday suppers. I always looked at the boys as my brothers. There were so many of us at family events that we always had a softball game going.

I was the only kid who was left handed and all we had were right handed gloves. So I had to learn to play softball using my right hand because they wouldn't buy me a glove. Such a small thing but even back then I was learning to adapt and overcome.

I spent a lot of time playing outside in the woods and creeks around the house. It was a good life, a good childhood for a time. I was able to go outside and run free, play and enjoy nature. My seven brothers and sister kept me really busy. I was a 'jump on a bicycle 'kid, never a Barbie doll type.

Attending school started to become a problem. My little brother and sister both had learning disabilities and were in special education classes. Lila would punish them because they would come home with bad report cards. I felt really bad about that. I wouldn't get punished because I was a B student. I didn't want to feel separated or alienated from them so I started letting my grades slide. That way, I figured, I would get punished too. I was always very protective of them.

My grades dropped to low C's for a couple of years. When I graduated middle school I went to Mary Jean Montgomery High School. I wasn't active in sports but played tenor saxophone in the band. I loved going to school, learning about business, writing, getting an education. I loved to type and I learned shorthand. The teachers were great. It was back in the day when schools were starting to integrate. So we had a mixture of races and exchange students as well, a very nice mix in the community. We were unified as a school, it was very nice. I never joined one group of kids, never joined a clique. I had one really good friend and we hung out together.

I didn't feel comfortable joining a group because of the circumstances going on at home, my mom and dad both being alcoholics, I didn't want anyone coming to my house to meet them.

This was always on my mind. I felt it was safer to stay to myself so I did. A couple of my brothers were problems as well. They were always yelling and screaming and being physical. I didn't tell anybody but when my dad remarried and we all moved in together at the age of seven, one of my brothers started molesting me.

I didn't want other kids to know any of this. I was traumatized, scared, hurt and alone so I began to focus on taking care of my brother and sister. That became my main agenda, to protect them and keep them from having to go through the things I was going through. It was horrible, so bad that I was ashamed. I didn't want other kids to not like me. I thought they wouldn't like me because of what was happening to me. I thought maybe it was my fault, maybe something I did to cause this to happen. It was a struggle and the struggle became a normal part of my daily life.

During this time, Lila gave up alcohol and became sober. She began to teach Sunday school and she would take us all to church. Except for my dad, he wouldn't go. Church became an escape for me, I absolutely loved the environment, I loved being there, the teaching of the Gospels, the singing. I was enthralled with the peace that I found inside the sanctuary to the point where a lot of times and because it was close to our house, I would walk to the church and go inside for the solitude. I get chills and bumps right now thinking about opening those sanctuary doors and looking in and being the only one standing there. It is very emotional for me now thinking about the peace I experienced by just walking into the sanctuary. I really loved being at the church so I went a lot and it became an area of escape from the horrible reality I was living.

Then Lila had an accident when I was 11 years old. During an operation, she was dropped off the table and was paralyzed from the neck down for a whole year. When she came home, I took on the role of caregiver to her and mother to my brother and sister. I stayed extremely protective of them. The responsibility of getting my brother and sister off to school, cooking breakfast, cleaning house, all of that fell on me. I didn't have a choice, I had responsibilities at a very young age. It was hard. There wasn't a lot of playtime, running around and spending time with friends.

My dad was working in the Pascagoula, Mississippi shipyard and left the house at 3:00 am every day and I was left in charge of the house. It was about this time that I realized the church was where I needed to be because those people were genuine and loving. They were caring and I didn't have to pretend with them. I could go in there and I could laugh or I could cry.

At around the age of 14, I started staying summers with my good brother Mike, not the one who molested me, and his family in Birmingham. I call him my good brother. I watched his kids while he and his wife worked. Every summer I wanted to go and be at my brother Mike's house.

I realized through that experience that there was a whole new world outside of what I was surrounded by at home.

The third year, actually the third summer I was watching the kids, I got raped by a neighbor and as a result, I got pregnant. I never told anybody about the rape.

I returned home to Mobile after the summer ended and got ready to start my senior year in high school and my stepmom Lila, came to me one day and confronted me saying, "Something is wrong. You haven't had a menstrual cycle, I have been watching you. What's going on?" I told her I didn't know.

She took me to a doctor to find out. I had never been to a doctor, never had a physical exam.

After the exam, the doctor told her that I was pregnant. I was scared, scared to death. I didn't know what was going to happen. Up to that point I kind of thought I was pregnant but I was naive and didn't know a lot about those things. I hadn't been dating anybody, I didn't have a boyfriend so I really didn't understand it at all.

Lila told my dad I was pregnant and after everybody knew, I told them I wanted to keep the baby but Lila said no, absolutely not. She took me to an abortion clinic and when we got there, she told the doctor, "Do not use any pain medication because I want her to feel everything that's going on and I want her to know that her being a whore caused this."

After it was over, the doctor said that I would probably never have kids because when I was thrashing around, he cut my uterus. He told us he thought I wouldn't be able to carry a child in the future.

That event catapulted me into being a stronger, more independent person. I decided that I was never going to let anybody put me into a position like that again. I was terrorized and suffered a lot because of that abortion so I made a plan. I decided to get through high school, to graduate, then move out of the house. That became my goal, that was my focus and what I needed to do.

I graduated when I was 18 and about two weeks after that I took my stuff and left. I told myself all the things I thought I needed to hear. I had transportation, a car my uncle loaned me, I could come and go as I wanted, I'm an adult now I said to myself, 18 years old, I can make my own decisions. Because I had graduated high school, to my mind everything would now be okay. My plan was to make money, to pay for my own car insurance, to take care of myself. I'm going to do this. But the truth is that when I left, my life became absolutely humiliating, terrifying and crazy from that point on.

I felt strongly that I needed to get away from my family, from all the abuse. I ran because my life was not under my control and internally I was going through so much agony and pain that I felt shattered. I didn't tell anyone where I was going and that decision was the beginning of the downfall of everything in my life. I jumped from the frying pan straight into the fire. That wouldn't be the last time in my life that I did that.

The downward spiral began a couple of days after I made the move. I left Semmes and drove in my loaned car, a 1979 Ford Thunderbird, to Mobile, Alabama. I was planning on going to school to become a secretary. That was the idea but the part about me becoming a secretary never happened.

I was on my own and I didn't want my family to find me. I didn't keep connections at the church because I was scared someone would tell my family where I was. I didn't want that mess. I needed to stay away and make money but the church was the only thing that had kept me grounded. The church couldn't protect me then or take care of me so the hours I wasn't able to be in the sanctuary were hours I missed. I was really a lost soul.

Soon after getting to Mobile, I got a job working for a company on a commission only basis, selling briefcases and luggage door to door. If I sold something I got some money. I didn't know the company was a cover for a drug ring. I didn't have a place to stay, my boss knew this and he told me that he had a place, an apartment where I could live. Two other guys were living there but that wasn't a problem according to him because there was an extra bedroom. I could move in and continue to work for the company. I was naive, I believed him, didn't have a lot of choices so I accepted the offer but it was a bad decision, a very bad decision.

After I moved into the apartment, my boss shows up with the two guys and says, "This is the deal. We don't want you, we want your car, we need transportation. We don't care if you work or not, you are going to stay here and take care of the place." They said to me, "You have a car and we need the car." They told me the car was for road trips but I found out later they were using it for trafficking drugs.

The second day I was there I was given what I was told was lemonade but it was alcohol. I had never had a drink in my life. They got me drunk and four different men sexually assaulted me. I woke up a couple of days later not in my own bed and nobody was around. The apartment door was locked. I couldn't get out. I went to the balcony and tried to open the slider door but that was locked. I was alone and without any food. It was like a shop of horrors.

They took my car, locked me in the apartment without food or water and left me for dead. One of the men named Robin put locks on the cabinets, bolted the front door and just left me. This became a pattern, they showed up after their trips and then would leave for days at a time without giving me any food. They were starving me and I began to get very, very skinny. I lost so much weight that I looked like I was on drugs.

After some time, Robin began giving me a little bit of freedom. I was allowed to go out by the pool, I could go to the laundry room, I could do little things. One of the days when I was outside, I saw a high school friend in the parking lot and I flagged her down. She was shocked at my appearance but I didn't tell her what was going on, I was too ashamed. I needed help so I asked her to call my grandma and let her know I'm alive and OK. I talked Robin into letting me see my grandma. He warned me that they would check the mileage on the car and if it didn't square up with the distance to her house, they were going to kill me.

When I drove to see my grandma, she took one look at me and just lost it. She swore I was on drugs but I wasn't, I was being starved.

I got back to the apartment and told the guys that my grandma was very upset with my weight loss. So they started giving me a quarter a day and told me I could walk to Albertsons and get a pot pie. They warned me to walk there, get the pie, come directly back, cook it and eat it. That's all I could do. I told them a pot pie costs $.27 with tax and they said if you can't find two pennies between here and there you won't eat. So I had to borrow two pennies from someone or I had to find two pennies on the ground to add to the quarter so I could eat. Then I had to stack the pot pie pans one on top of the other to prove to the guys that these were what I was eating.

I thought about running away from this all the time but where could I go? I didn't have many choices. They then started letting me ride around with them to do jobs selling luggage and briefcases, going to different businesses and making sales. They would give me a duffel bag and tell me to walk into a business and sell it. If I sold it, they told me, I would get lunch.

Then one day Robin put me into the car and we drove to Jacksonville. Strange but true. I knew the company had an office in Jacksonville, so we made our way there and checked in for work.

For about six months my life got better. I was living with Robin. Then one day I walked into the office and there was a man I had never seen before with cowboy boots and a white polo shirt. He was so handsome, his name was Mike and he talked to me. He smiled and said, "Hi beautiful." I looked around and he says, "Yeah, I'm talking to you. We have been assigned to ride together today." I thought, "Oh no, what's going on here? Are they setting me up?"

And here in my life is where I jumped again from the frying pan into the fire. Things can always get better in life and life got better for just a minute. But because you think that something can't get worse, it's not true, it can always get worse.

Mike and I rode around that day in his little Dodge Ram truck. We rode and he played music and asked me questions. I had never heard Blue Oyster Cult before and he asked me what kind of music I liked. Here I am, 18 years old and I had never heard Rock and Roll music before and it was fun, really fun. He asked me if I had a boyfriend and I answered, "Yeah, um Robin is my boyfriend," even though Robin was the worst of the men who held me captive for so long. He then asked me if I wanted to be his girlfriend even though we had just met that morning. And I was, "What do you mean?" And he said, "You look very sad, you have beautiful blue eyes but they are sad. And I don't like seeing that look on your face." He asked me, "Why don't you leave Robin and run away with me?" and I answered that was just crazy. He said, "You have never done anything crazy?" I told him that I had.

When I said that, I was thinking about why I had left home. Again, he asked me if I had thought about running away from Robin and I told him I didn't have anywhere to run. He then said, "Run with me, come with me." I thought about it for a few weeks, it took me that long to decide, then I told him one day, "OK, I'll run."

He told me there was a big New Year's Eve party planned and that he would be there. That was going to be the time. He said, "I need you." We made a plan for me to run out the backdoor of the place where the party was being held. A friend of Michael's named Lenny came along with him to the party. His job was to distract Robin. The distraction would give me my chance.

During the party, when Robin was distracted, I ran out the backdoor and jumped in the car Mike was driving. We drove off to his parent's house. It was New Years Day, 1985. I literally jumped in a truck with a man I barely knew and started a whole new life. In my mind it was as if God had sent this man into my life to rescue me.

On January 20th, 1985, three weeks later, Michael and I got married. I was still 18. He was my savior. He was the one who saved me from all that was happening to me with Robin, all that I was enduring. He got me out of the circumstances. I didn't love him at first but I grew to love him very much. We had good times together. Excitement came back into my life. I wasn't being held captive anymore. I could do what I wanted to do and I was free, free to eat and it was like being released from jail. We went on adventures together. He loved to scuba dive and I loved the water so we spent time going to Key West as well as amusement parks. We did so many fun things together. He introduced me to music and took me to a Pink Floyd concert, plus a concert with those guys with the beards, ZZ Top. He opened doors into areas I had never experienced. I was young and it was exciting for me. I was finally happy and I fell in love with who he was. I was having fun.

We moved to Orlando, and I got a job. We stayed with my brother Mike and his family for three months to get on our feet, then we got our own place, a rented trailer and moved in. My husband introduced me to his army buddy and his wife and we hung out with them a lot, going with them on adventures like the Kennedy Space Center and Key West where we would pop a tent and camp.

I took some pictures when we were at the Kennedy Center and when I had some time, I took them to be developed. When I went to pick them up, the guy behind the counter said to me, "You need to be careful with these pictures," and he slid the pictures over to me. I was asking myself what he was talking about and I started thumbing through them and there were pictures of my husband snorting cocaine off a glass mirror. There were pictures of big blocks of marijuana and other drugs.

When I confronted Mike with the pictures things immediately started falling apart between us. His attitude toward me changed, he started treating me differently. He became a completely different person. This was all within six months of getting married. The man completely flipped on me. He told me, "You are such a stuck up, you never party," and things were never the same again. He was using drugs and alcohol daily.

I came home one day to find him snorting cocaine. He grabbed me by the throat, shoved me against the refrigerator and called me ugly. He told me I was gaining weight, I was fat and that I was disgusting. He told me he was not attracted to me anymore and that I needed to lose weight.

He told me he had quit his job and was now going to drive a taxi. From that point on he was constantly switching and changing jobs. He went from having a really good job to not wanting to work at all.

The verbal and physical abuse escalated. I wanted to kill myself. My brother Mike was still in Orlando and when I talked to him, I always told him, "Everything's fine, everything's fine." I didn't want to be a failure so I lied to him. I didn't want him to say, "Well, we told you so, you married him after knowing him only for three weeks." But Mike didn't know what was going on before I met my husband. Mike didn't know the type of situation I was in. I figured when I ran away from Robin that the relationship I was getting into would be better, anything would be better, but it wan't better. It got worse and worse.

We would go through times where Michael would disappear for days then come back and apologize. He would take me out to eat and tell me how much he loved me. He would tell me he would never do bad things again and that I was beautiful, that he loved me just the way I was. I thought it was just a hard time he was going through and I would forgive him. I told him that together we would make it work, we'll make it happen. I wanted our marriage to work.

Our relationship went on like this for years, back and forth, back and forth. I kept thinking during the entire time that there was something mentally wrong with me, that maybe I was bipolar and I wondered why I kept accepting all of the trouble. I asked myself constantly why I felt that all of this is what I deserved. I had no confidence in my ability to do what needed to be done, to walk away.

Then in mid June of 1989, the cops surrounded our home, beat in the door and arrested Michael. He had been at a laundromat, had pulled a knife on a woman and attempted to assault her. She ran away, got the license plate number of his car and called the police. I discovered that he had been stalking her for over a year.

Together we then went through a battle in the courts. I stayed with him. I worked three jobs to pay for the attorney to keep him from going to prison. Finally the trial ended and he was sentenced to four years of sexual deviant counseling and placed on four years probation. We separated, I moved out of our apartment and I got a new job with an insurance agency.

Michael started coming to my job, sometimes driving by, pulling into the parking lot, sitting in the car and watching me. He started begging me to come back. I was living in my own apartment and he was telling me he couldn't live without me, that if I didn't come back to him, he would kill himself. He told me he needed me in his life, so I went back to him and we got a house together.

After a couple of months living with him again, I found out I was pregnant. We had been married for over six years. For the nine months of my pregnancy it was good between us, we got along without too much turmoil. Our daughter Brandi was born August 15, 1991, and six months after she was born he said to me, "That's not my baby, you probably cheated on me." He was making plans to divorce me and he didn't want to pay child support.

"That's not my baby, she's not my child!" he told me repeatedly. "I'm going to leave you because I don't believe she's mine and I won't pay for a kid that can't possibly be mine. I want a divorce, I'm gone, you cheated on me." He added, "No actually, I'm not going, you're going and you're going to take your kid with you."

I didn't leave immediately and before I could move, I found I was pregnant again. When Michael found out he forced me to have an abortion. He told me "This is going to happen, you don't want to be a single mom with two kids." I had the abortion February of 1992, and was back at work in two days. I wasn't in a good state mentally. I was terrified and didn't know what to do. I suffered with a lot of depression during this time. I was scared and I didn't know how I was going to handle raising a baby by myself now that he was making me leave.

In March of 1992, I was still with Michael. He was playing mind games with me, telling me everything was going to be OK, that things were good between us. About three weeks after the abortion I was in the apartment sitting in a chair and he walked in and said, "You have to make a decision today and I am not taking no for an answer."

I asked him what he was talking about and he dropped an open phone book on my lap, Yellow Pages, and told me to pick an adoption attorney. He said, "You know your biological mother had mental health issues and you know you are really not fit to be a mother or raise a child, especially a child who is not mine. So we are going to give Brandi up for adoption and let someone raise her who will love her, take care of her and give her a good life." I lost it and started crying.

He took the phone book off my lap and smashed it in my face and said, "I'm not telling you again, pick one!" At this point, I didn't have any will of my own. I had gone through so much and now he told me he didn't love me, that he never loved me and that no one would ever want to be with me because I was fat, ugly and unattractive. I had a C-Section for the birth of my daughter and a scar went down the center of my stomach. He told me the scar made me hideous, that no one would ever be attracted to me again and this was my only choice.

I thought that if I did what he wanted at least my daughter would be OK, that she would have a good life, a family that loved her and she wouldn't have to have him as a father because he's saying that she isn't even his. And that was impossible, so without looking at the phone book I touched it. I didn't know who it was and he said, "We're calling them now." He made an appointment.

I had just gone back to work for GEICO and one day a female attorney calls me at work and tells me she needs my signature on an adoption paper. I asked her what she was talking about and she said, "You're husband was in here and he filed everything for foster care placement of your daughter and you need to come down and sign a piece of paper. Your husband dropped your daughter off earlier today and the foster family has taken her. But we need your signature. Your husband explained to us that mentally you are not alright, that you have issues and we are trying to leave you out of all this because of your issues. But we need your signature."

I went to her office and asked her where my child was. She told me again the foster family took my child. I said, "I didn't give permission for any of this." I didn't want any of this to happen. I told her to bring my child back to me. She said, "The person who took your child is a Judge and he has other foster children. They're all at a softball game out of town and your daughter is with them. There is no way we can get your daughter back here today. The soonest I can get her here is tomorrow morning." That would have been Saturday.

I don't know how I did it, I was a wreck but I drove to my brother Mike's house, opened the front door and everyone was all happy and my sister in law comes into the room and asks, "Where's the baby?" Lila my stepmom was in the house too because it was Mother's Day weekend. I lost it. I fell on the floor. I was hysterical. I couldn't talk, I was crying hard and about to throw up.

I had the business card of the attorney in my hand and my sister in law took it. She worked for the Sheriff's office and she tried to get information from me, asking me questions and I couldn't talk. I finally said, "They have Brandi!"

My sister in law called the number on the card, talked to the attorney and the attorney told her that Michael brought Brandi to the office, that the foster family picked her up but she was working to get her back into town the next day. My sister in law told her, "We will be in the office tomorrow at 7:00 am to get the baby. No one had permission to do this, no one had full permission to release this baby to a foster family. We want her back."

We went to the office the next morning and the foster family came and brought my baby back to me. Mike was really upset about all the wrong that was happening to me. He drove me to the house where I had been living with Michael.

We went inside and found Michael sitting in a chair. My brother immediately got in his face and told him, "We're here to get her stuff and the baby's stuff as well. Don't move, don't say anything at all, just sit there and leave us alone. You're not messin' with my sister anymore."

My husband left us alone while we got everything. We packed all of my stuff, left the house and drove back to Mike's house. My sister in law had been planning on driving Lila back to her home in Alabama but to help me out, Lila offered to take Brandi with her. In my mind that sounded good to me, she loved Brandi and I was tired, so tired. Brandi would be in good hands.

I couldn't take my life anymore. I wanted to end it. I then and there made a plan to kill myself. I was going to blow my brains out and let him find me. I figured he might feel bad that he pushed me to this point. A couple of weeks earlier I had bought a gun from a pawnshop, thinking that if I was going to move out of the house and live alone with Brandi in a tough part of Orlando, we needed protection.

A few days after things calmed down and Lila and Brandi were gone, I drove to Michael's house with the gun. Michael was at work. I went inside and was sitting in the house when he came home. I was holding the gun to my head. When he saw me he started laughing and said, "Oh my God, thank you, you fat pig. That would solve all my problems. Please go ahead and pull the trigger. I will call your mom and tell her you're dead." I blacked out and the next thing I know, I shot him four times. Oh my God. He was dead. I tried doing CPR. I called 911 and said, "I just shot my husband." I was doing CPR on him when the police and paramedics arrived.

I had dropped the gun in the living room. When the police got there, I sat in the chair while paramedics worked on him. The police were paying no attention to me. I reached down and picked the gun up off the floor, put it to my head and pulled the trigger. Nothing happened. The gun jammed and a police officer saw me and she knocked the gun out of my hand. She said, "Oh my God, what would I tell my mom if you had shot yourself. It would devastate her." She told me she knew me and her mom knew me because her mom had worked with me.

All I could think of was, "Why isn't the gun working? It just worked. Why isn't the gun working?" They put me in handcuffs, took me to the car and drove me to the county jail. They told me that my husband had died. I didn't understand what I was facing, I didn't know anything about prison or being locked up. I spent one year in jail waiting for my trial and during that time, I spent a lot of time in prayer, talking to God. God was my foundation. Remember, I was raised in the church.

What I didn't say previously was that my husband was an atheist, he didn't believe in God. So when I took Michael on as savior, as saving me from the conditions that I was existing in, he literally became my savior and God was not. He was replaced. When we were together, Michael told me that I couldn't have a Bible, that he didn't want a Bible in the house so following his demands, I didn't bring a Bible into the house. It took something tragic like this shooting for me to understand that even though I walked away from God, He hadn't walked away from me.

There were different instances in the county jail where God spoke clearly and plainly to me through other people. There is no other explanation but God. The first time happened when a woman stood up in a county jail church service and asked, "Who is Marianne?" I was the only Marianne there and she said, "God said for me to tell you to hold on, that He is here with you, He has not forgotten you and He hears your prayers."

After that, I took my case to trial. I was charged with premeditated first degree murder. I was not offered a plea bargain or a lesser amount of time. I was never offered anything less than a trial. God had His hand on me and I took my case to a jury trial. My trial lasted a little over a week and I was found guilty. I was sentenced to life in prison with a 25 year mandatory.

I remember that when I was sentenced, my first thoughts were about my daughter; please take care of her, take care of my daughter, love her the way I would have loved her, take care of her.

Please, please let me see her while I'm here. My brother Mike gave me his word he would honor my requests, and he kept it. He brought Brandi to the county jail on many occasions, and I watched her take her first steps.

I should say here that as soon as the trial was over, one of the jurors went to the Judge and said, "We didn't know that she would get sentenced to life in prison if we found her guilty." But it didn't matter because it was too late. I was going to prison.

Lowell Main Unit, Florida Department of Corrections, was where they put me. Mike brought Brandi to the prison regularly so I could see her. She and I developed a relationship, a bond. We talked on the phone and as well, had visits together. All that time she was growing up.

But I have to say that prison was not something I ever imagined. I was a total outsider. I made some really good friends inside over the years but in the beginning it was liked being dropped into a foreign country and not understanding the language. Prison life was difficult for me. I believed I could make it, I didn't believe I would die in prison. I believed that one day God would open the doors and He would allow me a second chance.

I worked hard every day. I became a law clerk, I did architectural drafting and I worked in the optical lab for 13 years. I did everything I could to improve myself with education and business classes. I took on anything and everything that was offered. I immersed myself and bettered myself every day because I knew when the day came I was to walk out of prison I was going to be a different person. I was not going to let someone control my life and take me again through the things I had been through.

The times my daughter came with Mike to visit me I saw she was getting older, growing, blossoming and I wanted nothing but the best for her. I wanted her to pick a career that she loved, one that would support and take care of her. I didn't want her to have to depend on anybody. I wanted her to be always able to take care of herself and to stand on her own two feet. That desire was always very important to me because growing up, I couldn't stand on my own two feet and that inability led me to the circumstances in my life I had to endure.

While I was in prison, the Jury members wrote three affidavits saying they were coerced into finding me guilty of first degree murder. Three of the members didn't want to find me guilty but they felt they were coerced. During the trial, one member was doing studies of some sort and another was an alcoholic woman who only wanted to go home and have a drink. But the jury was sequestered in a hotel and she couldn't go anywhere.

Those three affidavits meant nothing to the court. It meant nothing that three jury members felt they were coerced to find me guilty of first degree, premeditated murder. Nothing. So I knew at that point that I had to stand on my own two feet. So I stood on those feet for 27 years and 30 days in prison. I worked to be the best person I could be.

I worked on my communication skills. I worked on helping, guiding and educating other women. It broke my heart to see young girls coming into prison who were in the same situation that I had found myself in when I was younger. I mentored women and girls and talked to others, anything I could do to help anyone in need I did. I knew that I would go home one day, I just didn't know when. I am proud of all those who did better, who in that time of despair had purpose, yes and that purpose was always to build up and help someone else. My spirit was doing this because prison can break you or it can make you. It can break you down.

There are so many people incarcerated who rely on psychotropic medication to numb whatever it is they're feeling, whatever they're going through. Then there are others who want to study, get an education, move forward and go to school. You have to make a decision once you are locked up: do you do the time or do you want the time to do you. You must decide what you want to do and make good decisions. Great things can happen. But if you keep making bad decisions you're not going to get good results. Choose life just as I chose life and that gave me the courage to do 27 years and 30 days.

It's strange but you never know exactly your release date until it's almost there, so I had an interview before the Parole Commission. This is just after I was transferred to a faith and character-based dorm. They dropped me in classification from close custody to minimum custody in the blink of an eye, which was unheard of. The Officers sent me to a dorm to do a special, three year program. I finished it in two years, actually 17 months and after seven more months they came to me and said OK, we're releasing you in 30 days. 30 days. Imagine that.

How do I prepare to walk out in 30 days after almost 30 years in prison? It was overwhelming and also exciting because in prison you watch TV and you see the commercials and you see a Hardee's and you say, oh, I want one of those hamburgers. Or you see certain things and you get so excited. I was truly overwhelmed.

The day came for me to be released and my daughter and a friend had both sent me an outfit that I could wear. I had two to choose from and I didn't know what to do. It was overwhelming just to have to choose between two outfits to wear, so I picked one. Unfortunately, not the one my daughter sent me and I walk out of the gate and my daughter was there. She was twenty-seven years old, a registered nurse, single and she greets me. We walked to the car and drove to a McDonalds and I think she was getting a kick out of watching my reaction. I couldn't pick what

I wanted to eat, everything was so incredible, the sights, the sounds, the smells and excitement.

She paid with a little plastic card. Then she took me to Walmart and I was filled again with anxiety.

The year is now 2024 and I have been home for almost five years. I am on parole but I was invited as a volunteer to go back into the prison where I spent my time. I loved visiting so much that I continue to go back in and talk to the girls on a regular schedule. I also do live streaming into the Florida Women's Reception Center. Love you girls. I also speak regularly at Marion Correctional Institution and last year the girls voted me Speaker Of The Year. What an honor.

God has continued to move mountains in my life, He has restored my life tenfold. I have so much more going for me than before I went to prison. I am abundantly blessed and thankful and every day I wake up grateful that God has given me opportunities to move forward.

There is a side story to me getting out. It was hard getting a job when I was first released. Everywhere I went looking for a job they said, "Oh, domestic violence, that's a problem. We can't hire you." I got tired of that response. One day I went to a Lucky's Market, a little grocery store in Gainesville and I asked the owner after he said he couldn't hire me, "Are you the same guy you were 27 years ago?" He answered, "Oh no!" Then I asked him, "Then why does everyone think I'm the same person I was 27 years ago? I need one person to give me a chance and I promise I will not disappoint you." So long story short, I started working at Lucky's Market for $10/ hour part time. My first check was $149. It was incredible to get that first $149 check.

Another time, I was asked to give my testimony to a nonprofit organization called Jesus Infusion. I am a Board member today. They do incredible work with the women inside prisons who are about to get out. Nicole and Randy Dyson run the organization and are my mentors today. One day we were having a fundraiser, I was giving my testimony and when I finished, this gentleman walked up to me and said, "If I can ever do anything to help you, please let me know. I asked him who he was. He answered, "Keith Perry and I would like to give you a job one day." I didn't think anything of it. Then he called me and told me, "I don't have a job in office for you right now, so I am going to create one, I want you to work for me."

He owned Perry Roofing Contractors. I started work as a receptionist because I didn't know how to do anything else. I had never been on the internet, I didn't know what an email address was and I had just learned how to use a phone. Today, I am the coordinator for our residential department and I make a lot more than $10 per hour. I work with fantastic people and they gave me that second chance at life. So yes, State Senator Keith Perry is my boss.

I can't stop doing what I'm doing now because I love it. I don't know what doors God will open for me, I'm young at heart. I just turned 58 last week. I was 26 when I entered prison and now I feel that this is the beginning of my life. Whatever door God opens for me, I'm willing to walk through it. I love to travel. Last year I went to Las Vegas. I rented a Corvette and I drove my best friend Lisa to the Grand Canyon. Lisa is my bosom buddy, she did ten years in prison. She had a natural life sentence but she got out. Inside, she and I used to dream about going to the Grand Canyon together but she never thought that I would rent a Corvette and drive her there. But God is good, he wants us to prosper. His desire is to give us the desires of our heart. His plans are to prosper us and to give us hope for the future, His future. That is what He has done for me. 2 Timothy 4:7 says to all of us that we should fight the good fight, finish the race, keep the faith and I hold close to that scripture every day.

I haven't finished the race yet and I am telling all those who will listen, do not focus on what you don't have but focus on what you do have and make it the best thing it can be. Education is the key, take advantage of what is offered. Believe in yourself because in order to succeed you have to believe in yourself. It doesn't matter if someone doesn't like you, you have to like yourself.

What other people think of you is none of your business. Believe in yourself and believe in God and believe He is there for you. He walks everyday with you.

Since Marianne Van Dongen appeared on the Death Or Prison podcast, she appeared before The Florida Parole Commission on April 17, 2024. Her parole was terminated and she is now a completely free, God loving individual. She will continue her work visiting prisons and giving her testimony as well as working as an able and valued employee of Perry Roofing, Florida State Senator Keith Perry's company.

3

"Stay Away From That Kid!"

"Whence is this monstrousness? And to what end?" St. Augustine, *"The Confessions of St. Augustine"*

Timothy Kane is a man with a purpose; he is living a life dedicated to helping others make good decisions. After reading his story you will understand his dedication.

TIMOTHY KANE
Death Or Prison podcast, Numbers 79 and 81
25 years inside.

I was born just outside of Chicago, Illinois. My family moved to Florida by the time I turned seven. I have an older brother and sister and a younger brother and sister. I don't really have many memories of living in Chicago except for the snow and the schools I went to. My family landed in Hudson, Florida. My grandma had lived there for decades so my dad moved us to be closer to her.

I immediately made a lot of new friends. We lived in a house right off of a canal on the gulf so we had beach access. It was my dad's grandparent's old house and we were renting it from grandma. Because of the beach, I was always swimming, running around. There were a lot of kids who were my friends so life was kind of normal, not notably different than any other kid going to my school, Hudson Elementary.

My parents separated when I was about eleven and that's when things started to go wrong, my life became more topsy turvy. My parents were living in two different places and I found myself bouncing between each of them. If I didn't like what was going on with one, I could go to the other and avoid problems. If there was discipline coming from my mom, I could avoid the discipline by leaving and staying with my dad. That could go the other way also. I believe that situation led me into what I walked into.

With their separation, I witnessed a loss of structure in my life. My mom and dad were once a unit, now they weren't. For instance, dinner was a constant that I could depend on, that everything revolved around. But once my parents split, my mom went back to school while working a job so she was never really there for us kids. No more family dinners. I found myself parenting myself and as an eleven year old, twelve year old kid, that wasn't a healthy situation. Plus, when I was at my mom's house I had to watch my brother and sister. I was in charge.

When I was at my dad's house, I recognize now that he was trying to be my friend instead of my father, trying to pacify me for the little time he had instead of being someone telling me, teaching me what was right and what was wrong. I didn't get any of the guidance I needed and I began to have issues. I felt strongly it wasn't necessary to be home. Often, I found myself staying at friend's houses on weekends because I could run from the responsibility of having to be a baby sitter, a job I wasn't ready for and which I didn't want.

My parents were both raised in Catholic high schools in Chicago but neither one gravitated towards church. Christmas was Santa Claus and Easter was the Easter Bunny kind of belief. It wasn't taught us kids that God was our creator and someone to respect and believe in.

There were a couple of men in my life while growing up that looking back I have to stop and pay them respect. Two of my friends had dads who were Pastors of churches. One friend, Daniel Holbrook, had a father named Rusty who was coach for the football team I played on. Sometimes I would stay at Daniel's house on Saturday nights and then go to church with his family on Sunday. I recognized that Rusty was different and I really saw this after I got arrested. He was the only person besides my parents to come to the Juvenile Detention Center where I was locked up after my arrest. Rusty passed away a few years after I got arrested but looking back now, I do recognize him as the first man of God who actually spoke things of God into me.

By the age of twelve or thirteen, I had a habit of staying out weekends with my friends, one of whom was my codefendant, Bobby Gardner. I met Bobby at the bus stop near my house when I was about seven or eight. He was the same age as my older brother, about three years older than me. Bobby was one of the first in our neighborhood to get a Nintendo gaming system. It had just come out so it was nothing for me to drop everything after school, go to Bobby's house and spend time there until my mom or dad would tell me to come home. But I wouldn't mind them. I found myself more and more disobeying my parents. By the time I was twelve and my parents had split, I stayed more and more at Bobby's house over the weekends. His house was a hideaway for me. We weren't getting into trouble then but I look back and identify the time as an unhealthy situation for a kid to think he can do whatever he wants.

Remember that Bobby is three years older than me, he was fifteen, maybe sixteen and his mom was single, working a full time job and not in the house a lot. There wasn't much supervision, Bobby had a free rein and he was left to do whatever he saw fit. I think his mom started dating someone about the time the crime happened. But he had dropped out of school when he was around thirteen. I was still in school and living with my mother at the time. Her house was about ten or twelve miles away from Bobby's.

Super Bowl Sunday in 1992, January 26th, I was spending the weekend at Bobby's house along with three other kids he had over, one a 19 year old named Alvin, also a 16 and a 15 year old. I had just turned 14.

I had heard of Alvin before I ever met him which was probably six months before this all went down. He drove me home from school one day and dropped me off. My mom saw him just this once, realize my mom is not a spiritual person, she's not anything like that, but she saw him once and she told me, "Tim, I do not want you to ever hang out with that kid again. Stay away from him." This all happened about two months before the crime.

Sometime later after I gave my life to God, I realized that one of the first principles of the word of God, the first commandment with promise in the ten commandments, is to honor thy mother and father and thou shalt live long in the land. I couldn't see it then, I didn't know it, I basically didn't want to understand it but I can remember my mother telling me to stay away from Alvin. I wasn't a rebellious teen but I was not set up to receive what she was imparting to me: the protection of God.

So we were all at Bobby's house watching the Super Bowl and playing video games, just normal stuff for me. But Alvin was talking Bobby into breaking into a house with him. He wanted to steal some 'stuff.' He told Bobby he needed money to get his license. That's how he presented it. He told Bobby he was going to do it that night and he convinced Bobby to go along with him. We were all at Bobbys house so we all went along.

Alvin told us he had a specific house in mind because they had satellite equipment and a big boat on the water. He had picked the house intentionally. I thought I was just tagging along, I didn't think I was going to get into any trouble. With that decision, I participated in the act of a felony where two people died during the commission of the crime.

We all rode our bikes to the house Alvin had in mind. Alvin broke into the house by kicking down and breaking in the front door. But before that, even before we went into the house, the 16- and 15-year-old had told us they weren't going inside the house so a little drama then played out and that's what convinced me I had nowhere else to go. I lived 12 miles away, it's already night and it's a cold night in Florida, January 26 of 1992. I was thinking I couldn't make a 12-mile bike ride home. One of the kids, the 15-year-old, lived only a street away. The 16-year-old had recently got into some trouble. He said he wasn't going to do anything that would get him into trouble again because his parents would kill him, those were his exact words, so he left too.

Alvin was berating the two kids and I was feeling the pressure he's putting on them. I didn't know what was really going on but I said I would go. I felt I had nowhere else to go.

Going in with Bobby, I witnessed Alvin as he kicked in the front door and then quickly moved toward the back of the house. Immediately after the door was kicked open, I heard a man's voice say, "What's going on? Who's here? Who's out there?"

I crawled under a table and stayed there. That was my whole experience in this, hiding under a table. I watched Alvin as he confronted an elderly man in his mid to late fifties and his mother who was in her late seventies. Alvin put them on the floor like it was just going to be a robbery. I could tell Alvin was flustered. He didn't know what to do with the people. He started dialoguing with the man and his mother back and forth. I was a witness to all of this. It got quiet as Bobby and Alvin started conferring between themselves. I decided that I could get out from under the table because I wanted to leave. I crawled out and told Bobby and Alvin that I wanted to leave. Alvin said, "No. No one is going anywhere."

The man on the floor was named John Bowers and he was speaking to both Alvin and Bobby, telling them to take anything they wanted but to just leave. He said he wouldn't even call the police. He begged us to leave.

Alvin had in his hands a small shotgun that he had brought wrapped in a towel on the handlebars of his bike. I couldn't tell if there was anything on the bike until we got to the house.

Alvin said to Mr. Bowers, "You guys have already seen my face, no one is going anywhere." By this time I am overwhelmed so I just backed away from him toward the front door where we came in. Alvin then shot the man. I don't know if the gun jammed but he threw it down and there was a knife and they attacked the woman until she stopped moving. Then everything got silent.

Bobby and Alvin went to the back of the house and that's when I left, I ran as fast as I could out of the house. I ran to the end of the street where we had thrown our bikes in bushes on an empty lot. By the time I pulled my bike out from the snag of all the other bikes, I saw Alvin and Bobby coming up the street.

My first thought was to go back to Bobby's house. He lived not too far away. On my bike and going around a corner I ran into the 16-year-old and he stops me. He sees the look on my face, how I was freaked out and panicked and couldn't talk. He was asking me what happened when Alvin and Bobby came around the corner and caught up to us, and Alvin asks me where I was going. I couldn't answer.

Alvin tells us all, "Nobody is going home, we are all going to Bobby's house and then we'll go to somebody else's house." Everything felt like I was in a daze. But we went to Bobby's house, and they cleaned up and hid the gun. He then took us to another guy's house about a mile away near Hudson Beach and he started to boast and brag to the guy about what he did, and he says to the guy, "I told you I could do this" He then presents Mr. Bowers severed finger to show the guy he was for real.

There was someone else in the room, another kid who hears this, thank God, because he was courageous enough to tell his older brother what he had seen and heard. His older brother then went to check the house out and saw there was smoke coming out of it. Alvin and Bobby tried to set the house on fire so the brother called the fire department and the police. When the police arrived they discovered the bodies. This was around ten at night but by six the next morning Alvin had made us all go back to his house which was five or six miles away.

We were inside in the morning and the police surround the house and they were calling to us to come out with our hands up. Alvin found a way to hide in the attic under some insulation. But the rest of us came out. I came out willingly and felt as though I was being rescued by getting into a police car. I felt this was finally over but little did I know the nightmare was just beginning. The police began to question us on the spot but they soon realized our young ages and they were forbidden by law to ask us any more questions. They took us to the station, called our parents and asked them to come to the station because they needed our parents present since they were going to question us further.

It seemed like I was stuck in a dream, in one of those long hallways that you can't run fast enough to get out of. It seemed as though everything was in slow motion and yes, I felt completely overwhelmed from the minute I walked through the broken front door to the time I spent under the table hearing other people's voices, to the time I was in the police station and being questioned.

Getting arrested I felt I was getting saved. I wasn't around that guy Alvin, anymore. Under questioning I tried to tell the police what I saw. I answered the questions but I remember the shame and I knew there was some things I was leaving out because answering the questions made me feel like I was guilty too, like I went with those guys to that place and therefore I was one of them. I saw this all happening over and over in my mind, I was in the room, how did it all happen, how can this all be?

Once reality set it in, I knew shame, I felt terrible. I knew guilt when my parents saw me for the first time at the police station and they looked at me. I felt really bad. My mother didn't look at me the same way she always had. I was different in her eyes. I knew she wanted to hug me but she couldn't, that wasn't an option. I didn't know God and I didn't know how to reconcile what was going on. I felt completely alone and isolated.

I was locked up at the Juvenile Detention Center. At the Center, the first non-blurred moment I can recall is when Rusty Holbrook, the man I mentioned before, the Pastor, came to visit me. I remember how dark everything appeared to me before he came. I now realize that Rusty was a man filled with the Holy Spirit and he was speaking what God wanted me to know, that He loved me. Despite all that I had been part of and God being a God I didn't really know, I saw a glimmer of light. I didn't understand it but I saw a light in the midst of all that darkness. Rusty was the first person to make the blur go away. He planted a seed by speaking into me God's spirit. He put me in a place to listen and look for something related to God because I didn't know God. I didn't know which way to look to find God.

After a nine day stay at the Juvenile Detention Center, I was transferred to the County Jail where I was to be adjudicated and a date set for my trial as an adult. I stayed in County Jail for about two and a half years awaiting trial.

It was during this time I had a transformation. I finally came to the conclusion that I was guilty before God and my attorney told me in a way that I could understand, that the authorities could take away my life, that I was facing a life sentence. He explained what a felony murder was, that I was an active participant in a crime where two people died.

I didn't even have a life yet and at the age of 14, I didn't know what life was. And here, they were going to take it away. This attorney told me all of what could happen and I became despondent.

It was a little over a year after being arrested that I found myself sitting in this jail multipurpose room with a few other guys and there was a little old tattooed ex biker, a volunteer, telling us about the love of Jesus. The first thing that came to my mind was, "Why would this guy come talk to us?" If I were him, I figured I would be anywhere but here in this place but this guy volunteered to come see us.

Then with this tattooed biker I am seeing and hearing the message again through a complete stranger who's talking about Jesus, this guy Jesus. I was still a kid and prison was about to take away my whole life. This biker told us how God had delivered him from his addictions, drugs and alcohol, how he was abused and how he inflicted his abuse on others as he got older. But God had changed him through Jesus and he told us we needed to know about Jesus. He made sure we all had Bibles before he left that day. He told us that if we ever had questions about this guy Jesus, we could start with the book of Matthew. We could read the story for ourselves.

So God set up a circumstance. It wasn't but about a month or two later that I found myself getting put into a solitary confinement cell alone for 45 days. I didn't do anything wrong, it was a complete set up but there I was. God wanted me to be by myself for this time. Immediately I felt the walls closing in on me in a six by eight cell.

I'm fifteen years old then and my lawyer had been telling me how the legal system worked and how I was going to be convicted. The illusion of possibly going home had completely vanished. The guilt and distress I then felt became more substantial.

I looked in my cell's bin and the Bible the biker gave me was the only thing I had to read. I remembered the man spoke about Jesus and answers. I had no other distractions, no view of the outside, no one to talk to so I read it.

I opened the Bible for the first time and I flipped around until I found the book of Matthew and I started reading. I didn't understand a lot of what I was reading, a lot of the language, but immediately I recognized something different in Jesus. Reading through Matthew, Mark and Luke, I didn't really understand what was going on, the dynamic of what was happening. I comprehended everything I was reading but I didn't understand the reason for Jesus being killed. He's such a good guy, he's doing good things, great amazing miracles, and yet he's still being put to death. I didn't understand why people hated him so much. The story didn't make sense to me until I read the book of John.

When I got to John's Gospel, I realized that when Jesus was about to go to the cross, He didn't belong there, I belonged there, and that's when something changed in me; I perceived that He was willing to lay down his life for me. I was guilty, yet He was willing to go to the cross for me. He took my place. Since that day, September 12, 1993, when I discovered all of this, I would never be the same. His resurrection made sense to me. I lit up with joy knowing I had an eternal life with Him. My heart was free. I never had known real freedom before this, I was learning about bondage daily but I knew that even if my life was taken, it's a drop in the bucket compared to eternity. Because of what Jesus had given me, I knew that if I had to spend the rest of my life in prison, and I say this even now after spending twenty five years of my life behind bars, if I had to do another twenty or even fifty, Jesus was worth it.

The day of my trial finally rolled around but because I was such a kid, I was oblivious to how it all impacted everyone around me. I was so caught up in my mess I couldn't see outside of my own circle until the day of my sentencing. It was that day I realized it wasn't just about me. Because I felt guilty and had thought about being convicted, I was prepared for the sentence but my parents and my grandmother who was in the court room with them, weren't. My parents and grandmother cried. Feeling their grief that day hurt me more than the Judge's sentence and what he said: Two life sentences with a minimum mandatory of 25 years each, to run concurrently and no parole eligibility until I had done 25 years. It was a life sentence for two Capital Murders.

When I was transported from County Jail to Lake Butler's North Florida Reception Center after my sentencing, the first thing I noticed was that I was allowed outside, which for me was a big deal because I felt like I had been stuck in a dungeon until this time. Prison was night and day better than the conditions I had gone through for the last two and a half years in County Jail.

I stuck out as different because of my young age, not only to the inmates but the guards also. When I was going through the transfer center, some of the guards pulled me out of line and either grilled me or belittled me with questions like, "What's a boy doing here in my prison?" I must have heard that question ten times the first two weeks I was in Butler. I turned to God for the answer because I didn't have one.

I told them I didn't know why I was there but in my mind I knew where I was going. I had to change the focus from where I had been. I wasn't the same guy in the confinement cell, there's something new here, inside me. It was resurrection power. I was out of close management and walking freely. I felt liberty even in the prison. I could talk to people without the weight I once had, the weight of no communication with God. I now knew God and I was learning more and more every day about Him. I was unbound.

Since I had no background in a church I didn't know about church services in the Chapel. I didn't know I was supposed to be there. I was green to everything. Then I met a Panamanian guy, Alfonso Anderson. He was from New York and was in my dormitory, a dorm set up for guys 21 and younger. We were under the child nutrition program where the prison made sure we had milk for lunch. That was the only difference between us and the rest of the compound. We ate first for breakfast and lunch because of our dietary needs but that regulation was the only thing that separated us from the adults. All of our other activities were on the compound, work, recreation, all of that.

Alfonso was getting out in a few months and he obviously had the Spirit. He stopped me once and asked me a couple of hard, pointed questions about God. I didn't know this guy from Adam but he says to me I want you to come to my bunk tonight and I'm going to show you some things from the Bible. I went that night and he began to disciple me for the last five or six months of his time. He got me reading the Bible and into a Bible study. He prayed with me and introduced me to some guys at the Chapel. I soon got baptized and got involved in some of the programs offered. I got involved in the choir and I felt like I was growing leaps and bounds in the knowledge of God because I was devouring the word of God, reading it all the time. I couldn't wait for the count to end so I could bet back to reading the Bible. When I was away from the Bible I couldn't wait to get back to the story, especially if I was reading the Old Testament.

During this time, one night I had a dream about Moses taking the children of Israel to fiery Mount Sinai. I told Alfonso about the dream and he told me, "Now is the time. We are going to fast and pray for you and you are going to receive the Holy Spirit." I had been baptized the week before and another brother who was part of our Bible study joined us in the fast.

Fasting in prison is not allowed as a juvenile but God had grace on us and we were able to fast. The day this was all supposed to happen, we went to the recreation field, prayed together and suddenly Alfonso starts praying and speaking in tongues. I had never heard anything like this before so it baffled me. Then he begins to translate and the next thing I know, I hear the Lord speak and say to me, "Walk with me, I am coming soon." I hear this, I'm shocked, I find myself on the ground and Alfonso is helping me up.

Alfonso tells me that the Lord imparted a gift to me. The Holy Spirit he said, "Gives you the gift of wisdom." In hind site I marvel because I am 16 years old, in an adult prison and with that wisdom I ended up going through my entire prison experience with no marks on my disciplinary record. God gave me wisdom to get involved in the right programs and to associate with the right people. I always put God first in my decisions. In the book of Proverbs, it says the fear of God is the beginning of wisdom. I respected God. I had been an offense to God in my previous life and I never wanted to do anything like that again. I made sure that I didn't mess up because I realized how careless I was that night and how it caused so many people so much pain. I hurt my family, hurt everyone that was in my life, everyone who was associated with me, so I began putting God first in my thoughts and the processing of everything. My decision-making process changed forever.

I tried to live my life to the best of my ability. I got transferred to Apalachee Correctional, and became part of the Chapel crew under Chaplain Hunter. Up to that point in my life, I wasn't put into any school program to continue my education. I had been a freshman in high school when I got arrested and they hadn't allowed me to take the GED in County Jail but in the Department of Corrections it was a different story. I had scored high on tests that were given me and after the tests, they put me into morning educational programs. I worked in food service in the afternoon.

I was working Sundays and Chaplain Hunter noticed I wasn't attending services anymore. He saw me working the chow hall one day and he asked me why I hadn't been coming to services. I said, "Sir, you see where I am working, this is my job assignment." He understood the situation and told me he wanted me to come work for him. That way he could make sure I was at every service. Imagine that. I was now 17 years old and the Chaplain wanted me to come to work for him, he wanted me there with him.

That blew me away because I wasn't trying to be on anyone's radar. It wasn't too long after I started work for him that Dateline NBC contacted me and asked me if I would do an interview. I agreed and Chaplain Hunter was in the room when I did the interview. I knew in my heart God made that happen, that this was a God thing. It was like a whirlwind hit me.

They interviewed me for three hours and of course I said a lot about Jesus. After it was aired, I got transferred to Hardy Correctional. I hadn't put in for a transfer but again it was another God thing because I was moved closer to my family.

The Dateline episode came out and all of a sudden I started getting scores of letters. God spoke very clearly to me that I had to respond to each and every one. Here I am, 18 years old now, and I don't even have stamps but God made me a witness for what He did in my life because I never ran out of stamps. People sent me books of stamps so I could respond to the letters. God began to make me a witness for what He was doing in my life. I was able to help people work out their own salvation just because they marveled at this kid in prison who met Jesus in a confinement cell and they wanted to hear all about it. God had set this up and I saw His hand in all of it.

One man who wrote me for a few years was from Nashville, Tennessee. His name is Ron Miller and he told me in one of his letters that he wanted to visit me, that he had a home in the Tampa Bay Area and he was close by. I didn't have a problem with that so I got him a visitation application and he came. That's when a friendship started that still continues to this day.

In the visit, he told me he had a lot of influential friends who were musicians who would enjoy putting on a concert for the guys. I didn't know what he meant by that, I had never seen a concert. But over the next few years, Ron formed a charity called Timothy's Gift, a prison music ministry that's still in operation. They have done major tours with named musicians from Nashville in many prisons since their start. It's amazing to believe that I got a witness from God that my life was impacting something outside the walls, not just in my cell and my small sphere, but that God had made something out of my mess. Ron brings God's message inside and named his ministry after me, Timothy's Gift. That freaked me out, at first I was not cool with it because I didn't want anyone to believe that I was someone special. I am not, Jesus is. As long as Jesus was exemplified and lifted up then I was cool with it. But I wasn't cool being in a spotlight. I wanted to fly under the radar as I've said.

Just about this time in my life, I started hearing news about my younger brother and sister falling into trouble. I heard echos of what was going on in my mom's life, her struggle to hold things together, especially after what I had put her through. When I talked to my family I had to be careful talking about Jesus, for to them I sounded like a crazy man. I didn't want to preach to them. I knew the power of the resurrection and I wanted them to know it, how it can transform so I had to be careful when I talked to them. I wanted them to know the liberty I had because they didn't have it. They weren't free and I could see how 'not free' they really were. Then my mom passed away while I was inside. I was in Sumter Correctional, it was 2002, and I had been in for 10 years.

With her passing came the biggest, hardest regret I ever had because she didn't recognize the freedom that was in me. She had worried so much about me that I put her over the edge to where she went downhill fast. Her health deteriorated while I was inside. She began abusing her prescription medications and drank until her end. Her death burdened me so much to see the effects of my sin play out in her life and in my family's.

Eventually my interview for review for a parole hearing was scheduled for 2017, about one year before my mandatory sentence of 25 ended. I had no idea what would happen or what was to come out of it. The man who did my scoring on a matrix comes up with a date of 2027 for my release and he tells me that this is what he is recommending based upon the charges and all the things involved in the case. That date would be another ten years that I would have to do.

I went back to my dorm praying to God. It wasn't that I couldn't do another ten years but that my family couldn't handle another ten. I was crying out to God.

I called my father and told him about the scheduled parole hearing and he told me he couldn't drive 4 hours to Tallahassee because he didn't want another disappointment. I knew what he was talking about. Something immediately made me tell him, "You have to go, you have to go." It wasn't me telling him this, I knew it was God. My dad had been to every court date I'd ever had. He experienced so much disappointment he didn't want more. But I knew that God was going to do something and He did.

The hearing was held and the sitting District Attorney from Pasco Pinellas, Florida, Bernie McCabe, was in attendance. All the people in the room and the people who were representing me, recognized him and thought he would speak in opposition to my release. I wasn't at the hearing but I was told all of this later.

The floor opened for statements and Mr. McCabe was first to speak. He told the commission how he felt, that if this sentencing was handled properly 25 years ago, we wouldn't be here today. He said, "I pray the commission has mercy and lets Timothy out as soon as possible." He then sat down. All of my family's jaws dropped and they were all asking themselves, "What just happened?"

One of the Commissioners then said, "We have never had a sitting District Attorney in any form or fashion, come and speak on behalf of a man who is in prison for murder." The Commission then agreed to my release and set my date for as soon as possible after my mandatory was completed which was another six months.

When I called home to hear the news because I wasn't in attendance, I didn't know how to take all this in. I thought I was going to be set for a 2027 release but now I had only six more months to do. My sister told me that my attorney didn't want me to tell anyone but that was impossible because when I made the call from the prison phone I had ten people behind me, all praying for me. My family didn't grasp what prison life was for me. I had brothers with me inside that I knew better than my own family. We were all in the family of God and I had a real kinship with them. God was with us all.

My end of sentence occurred February 23, 2017. I walked out of Everglades Correctional Institution. Today, seven years later, I am preaching at the prison where I spent 18 years, in that very same Chapel where God spoke His word to me and told me that I would speak to the fences and tell them to come down. I walk through and across those same fences today on a regular basis. It shakes me up to know how good God is. Today, in 2024, free for more than seven years, I get to tell my story, I get to go back and witness to the guys. I surprise them with my story and I am able to tell them that there is a God and He loves guys in blues.

If there is one thing I could say to all those men and women who will read this is that Jesus said after His resurrection and before He ascended to heaven, all authority, not some, but all authority, had been given to Him. I was a kid when I first heard those words but I believed and I am telling you, the demonstration of His power throughout my life shows He has the final say in everything concerning you. Everything. Turn to Him, trust Him and you will never be disappointed. Put your life into His hands and He will bless it to the point where you see the impact you can have not only on other people's lives but especially on eternity.

Today Timothy Kane is living the life God has called him to lead. He owns a small company, has his own family, works with Timothy's Gift Prison Ministry and goes regularly into prisons where he brings his testimony of the power of God's love and redemption to the incarcerated. Alvin Morton remains on Death Row. Bobby Gardner has another 18 years to serve before he is eligible for parole. To support Timothy's Gift Prison Ministry, please visit timothysgift.com and donate.

4

"Darwin, I Did This For You"

"For in this hope we are saved; but hope that is seen is no hope at all. Who hopes for what he can already see?" Romans 8:24

Not many people get to see Jesus face to face. Darwin "Casey" Diaz is one of the chosen ones. He grew up in Los Angeles, California, and at the tender age of eleven, was jumped into one of the most notorious gangs in his neighborhood. Eventually he earned the title "Shot Caller," which meant he had the power of life or death over rivals at the tip of his tongue. While he was locked in solitary confinement for a murder he had committed, he had a visit one day…

DARWIN "CASEY" DIAZ
Death Or Prison podcast, Numbers 10, 11, 12, 13.
13 years inside.

I was born in El Salvador, Central America, and was brought to the United States at the age of two. My family moved to Southern California, the Rampart District of Los Angeles, not too far from South Central. El Salvador at that time was in political mayhem. Violence was everywhere. The people were in the first stages of what would become a civil war. My grandfather on my father's side was in the military and he and my grandmother were both executed in front of their children, my father being one of them.

I think this tragedy had something to do with who my father became later in life. It influenced both his childhood and adulthood. He became violently abusive toward my mother, often physically assaulting her in our home. Toward me, the abuse was more verbal and emotional. I was a child but he had a way of making me feel less than I was when I was around him. He carried himself like that for a very long time and the abuse definitely did something to my psyche. I really disliked being at home because of my dad's violence.

My relationship with my mom, however, was great. I looked forward to Sundays because that was the only day she didn't work and early on as a young child, we would go to the laundry together, taking a little basket with all our clothes and spending quality time together. To this day I have a wonderful relationship with my mom. She taught me the value of hard work because she was the example of someone who didn't want a government handout or assistance of any kind. She was against taking money if she didn't work for it.

I remember one time in particular, we fell on a hard time economically, something was going on and we had to get assistance for a very short time. She sat me down and told me that this "is not the right thing to do." I didn't understand all the ins and outs of what she was saying but I knew it was important for me to know. I was probably seven or eight years old and she told me that this wasn't the way it was supposed to go down, that we are supposed to work for our money. She always talked to me as if I was an adult and she made sure that I knew she was going back to work because, "We were no longer needing the money and everything was going to be fine, it was soon going to be back to normal."

We had many talks like that in the form of an adult conversation because she didn't spare me details when we talked. She is a sharp, straightforward person and I believe that her manner has helped me immensely, immensely all along my walk.

I knew at a young age that my mom was the one providing food and comfort. She was the one responsible for putting the roof over our heads. She was short of five feet and after working two jobs and spending an outrageous number of hours working, she would come home and get beaten by my dad. He would beat her as a man would beat another man.

Watching this did a number on me and it contributed to me looking at life differently than the average kid. I grew to have no concern for life or property. And I think this situation at home was one of the many predisposing factors in my life to make me join a gang. The attractions to gang life were a sense of belonging and feeling a false sense of family. As a kid, I was for the most part left unsupervised and like many gang members, I was raised basically in a one parent system. That's a very unfortunate truth for many today because that's not how God designed the family, it's not supposed to be that way.

In my case, a father was present but because he was brutally violent, his violence influenced how I thought, how I walked, how I dealt with problems and especially how I dealt with people in the long run. It's a recipe for disaster when the house isn't in order. So for me, the gang culture embraced me and I embraced it. Because of the feeling of family within the gang, I think the sense of belonging lured me into getting more and more involved with the culture and the gang thinking.

My gang life began when I was jumped into the Rockwood Street Locos at age eleven. In Southern California there are two different ways gangs initiate new members. One of the ways is they put you in the middle of several members and then they just jump you, assault you, beat you and they count to thirty seconds while the are doing it. The other way is for them to spell out the gang name while they are beating you. For me it was the thirty second count. They were beating me and I was fighting back as hard as I could. Once the time is over, or they are done spelling out the gang name, you are then officially in, you're a member and it's handshakes all around, hugs and pats on the back. Hopefully when it's all over there aren't too many missing teeth. That's how it rolls.

I got jumped in by three guys. Later on, one of them was murdered, another committed murder and the third guy got involved in organized crime. I have an eleven year old son now and fortunately he is oblivious to that lifestyle.

After I was in, I started learning about the gang drug business. There is definitely a business side of any organized gang but drugs didn't do anything for me personally, drugs weren't attractive to me. I did a taste test of probably everything and I saw what drugs did to other homeboys but drugs just weren't my thing. I didn't see the purpose of drugs. For me violence was my addiction, that's where I really got involved.

I remember the first violent crime I committed was with one of the individuals who jumped me in. We had stolen a car and we were driving through alleys very, very fast. Los Angeles has a lot of alleys and we were flying through them, he had the pedal down and we were almost getting airborne at times. I thought at one point we were going to crash and that would be the end of it. At some time, we crossed over into a rival gangs territory.

He had problems with someone in that area and he wanted to take care of him. We found the guy and he was by himself. We jumped him and he proceeded to stab him with a screwdriver many times. He calmly handed me the screwdriver and said, "It's your turn," so I stabbed the guy. I was eleven years old and that stabbing was my first. I don't know how much damage I did being eleven but that was my first act of violence against another human being. I regret that to this day.

The whole thing was pretty brutal but that act made a name for me. From then on I carried screwdriver in my back pocket. If it wasn't the screwdriver, it was an icepick. Those were my weapons.

The drive-by shooting was happening in the 1980's and 90's. That was the iconic violence back then, but for me, I saw drive-by's as too easy. You get a gun, get in a car, turn the lights off and do a drive by. Not for me. I was the extreme type right out of the gate.

What I am about to tell you is not to glorify what I did as a youth because I followed an extremely violent pathway. The purpose of the following is to show the depth of evil to which I had sunk and to compare that evil with whom I am today, only through the mercy and love of God.

My thing was to walk into a rival gang's territory, chase down a guy and face to face, do to him what I thought needed to be done. The violence I was committing really put me out there and after a while, I started to hear my name mentioned more and more in the streets. I began to see myself as a leader. My young ego got stroked and I wanted more recognition. I wanted to get to that penitentiary everybody talked about. Weirdly, I believed that I needed prison time to make me somebody. I wanted to make sure my name was known, that's how desperately wicked my heart was, very, very dark, but for me it was just the thing to do.

I strived for acceptance, I wanted the leadership role and I ended up in the circles of older gang members, gang leaders. Early on, I stayed away from the members who pretty much didn't do anything, they just dressed the part, they looked the part. They were there for the girls or whatever reason they made up. But when it came down to the nitty gritty, when the action was on, they were nowhere to be found. That inaction wasn't for me.

For whatever reason, the older members took me under their wings and I ended up in their meetings. That's a real recipe for disaster for a young, impressionable boy. This acceptance contributed to many of the actions I took later in my life, especially the way I carried myself when I was around other gang members. I had recognition, pats on the back from older guys who validated me and made sure everyone around accepted and was happy for me. That does something to a young kid's emotional stability very fast.

One guy influenced me more than anyone else. He was fifteen years old, not much older than me at the time but old enough to be recognized. He was very violent and highly respected on the streets of Los Angeles and his name was being tossed all over the place. He was considered to have a good name and everyone had a lot of respect for the guy, and he's only fifteen and I'm with him. With violence we were putting our names out there.

My gang, the Rockwood Street Locos, shared part of our territory with another rival gang, 18th Street. They were very large at the time. The news media had them all over television sets and in many news articles. Many of our members had cousins, brothers, fathers and sisters who belonged to 18th Street. I started being sentenced to Juvenile Hall when I was about eleven and I saw many of them inside. Many were snitching. I didn't like that, I didn't like what I saw. So very early on, even though we were getting along with them, I began giving them trouble.

What I disliked is that people in the media and people in our hood, made them sound as if they were this huge gang that had a lot of power, a lot of strength and that they were highly organized. My goal became the question: how do I take these dudes down? What do I do to make a name for Rockwood and for me?

I picked up the phone, called one of my real solid dudes, then called a meeting with some of the guys. I tossed the idea that I wanted to make a move on 18th Street. I wanted to really do a number on them. They had a clique in their gang calling themselves Colombia Little Cyclones and if you were in 18th Street, you wanted to be part of that clique. They were down the street from us. We shared our neighborhood with them as well as a lot of landscape outside our neighborhood, probably about a ten mile radius. Our clique could walk to one of their cliques without problems, we were fine with each other. They had their older guys, some thirty or forty years old which made them look like they had it together and for me, a young gang member who was trying to make his stripes, that was the perfect setup, the kind of thing where it was, "Let's do this, let's role on 'em and make a name for ourselves."

About six or eight gang members showed up to my apartment when I tossed the idea. I remember one guy who was there had three brothers in 18th Street. This guy was eventually killed by LAPD Rampart. I told everybody we were going to make a move, that our clique was going to be the clique to make the move regardless of what everyone else in Rockwood said. We were calling the shots on this and this is why we are having this meeting.

The guy says with a puzzled look on his face, "You know I have three brothers in 18th Street. What are we going to do if we run into any of my brothers?" It got really quiet in the room and I didn't even flinch. I said, "If we run into any of your brothers, we're going to take 'em out. That's that. You have a problem with that? You've got to let us know right now."

He looked like he wanted to say something but he didn't. Unfortunately two of his brothers were later murdered by Rockwood. The move we made was pivotal in our culture and boosted my name on the streets throughout Los Angeles. Everyone knew it was me who made the call and me who organized it and made it happen.

Unfortunately it became a bloodbath within the ten mile radius. We had access to guns through sellers and through burglaries so they were easy to get. Most of the time I wasn't carrying a gun, just the screwdriver.

But on one particular occasion I was out with a couple of guys not looking for trouble but trouble found me. I was in a little mama papa burger, chicken joint having a meal and some individuals from 18th street saw us, jumped us and a fight ensued.

I had a sawed-off shotgun under a seat in my vehicle parked outside and I ran to it. One of the guys was chasing me with a heavy crowbar, a thick metal one. We got to my car and I pulled the shotgun from beneath the seat. It was already loaded, a one-shot shotgun with a hammer and when I turn around he was about to hit me. He was launching the crowbar at me. I fired. The first shot killed him. I shot him in the face.

When someone gets shot from that short range, how do I say, today I wish I could erase the memory, rewind the clock and start that time all over for both my victim and me. But then it was a different time. He fell outside my car door. I reloaded and proceeded to shoot him four more times.

It was broad daylight. I ran. I say this now with a lot of sorrow and emotion and as a Believer, I think of someone's life being lost, a fellow human being. Someone lost a son regardless of the circumstances. I remember, I don't forget. But at that time I was so used to the violence that I was desensitized, my heart was calloused, my heart was wax cold at that moment. I didn't care about life, it was cheap and had no value.

I know I am forgiven through Jesus Christ but even knowing that, I have remorse, it's an awful thing to live with, this human flesh and I wish I had done a lot of things differently. My wish? That I had never got involved in a life of crime and of gangs, I regret it, I really do.

But now, the police were looking for me. I was able to avoid arrest for 21 days. Initially, I was housed in one of my homeboys' apartments. His mom hid me. I also lived in an abandoned apartment for a short time.

Then on a Friday, two other gang members of mine and I were eating at a newly opened Chinese restaurant. I happened to have two firearms on me and bullets in my pocket. We were talking about throwing a party that night. Another gang member we got along with from another gang, shows up to meet me. After we ate, and I don't know why to this day, but for some odd reason I took the two handguns and gave them to the guy and jokingly said, "Be careful you don't get caught with them, one of them is hot," suggesting that I had used one. He laughed and gave me some money and told me that he would "pick me up tonight."

It was a very short meeting, maybe five minutes at the most, and when we left, one of my guys jokingly said, "You know there's a helicopter up there and it's for you." We all laughed and we started walking northbound on Normandie, up the hill toward Oakwood. We made a right on Oakwood and sat on the stairs of an apartment building and everything started to happen fast. LAPD Homicide and a special unit came down on us like a sea, guns pointed at us. I briefly thought of jumping a wall but I didn't. They put us on the floor. I didn't resist arrest but I thought it interesting that they hogtied me.

They threw me into the backseat of an unmarked vehicle and took me back to the corner of Normandie. They hauled me out of the car like I was a gym bag, a suitcase, and put me on the pavement. I listened and heard their handheld walkie talkies talking about the arrest. I would later find out that it was a teacher who knew I was wanted, who recognized me when I was walking to the Chinese food restaurant, pulled over and made the 911 call.

The Police took me to Rampart Division where I was processed, then because I was 15 years old about to turn 16, they took me to East Lake Juvenile Hall. This was where I spent my time waiting to be arraigned then go to trial.

I remember some interesting talks with Detectives from Rampart Robbery Homicide. They asked me if I had any information on any of my homeboys, that if I did and was willing to share it, they could work out some sort of deal where I could avoid being tried as an adult. I remember very clearly telling them that I had nothing to say. They didn't stay long because I think they realized very quickly that they weren't going to get anything out of me. They left their phone number on a card on the table, told me that if I changed my mind I could call them and then they walked out of the interview room.

About this same time, California decided to get tough on gang violence. I was placed into the initial batch of young offenders who would be tried as an adult. If you ask any gang member who was tried at that time as an adult, they would tell you they just didn't care. I didn't care.

I was found fit to start the whole process and to be sent to an adult prison if convicted. I was facing 2nd Degree Murder charges and additionally, fifty two counts of armed robbery.

I was running pretty violently for all the time prior to this. As a young gang member, I had been arrested many times and placed in Juvenile facilities, Camp Miller and Los Padrinos for example. I had done the tour of the Juvenile Hall system of California, I was familiar with it and not intimidated, California had a history of being very lenient in sentencing. I have to say that if I had committed my crimes in any other state I know for certain I wouldn't be out walking free today.

I was hardened even though I was still young. They told me I was going to be tried as an adult but I didn't care, I had total disregard for the law. I showed no emotion and the outcome of the trial really didn't matter to me. I remembered a couple guys who were with me through the Juvenile system and who did similar crimes, they had similar cases. One guy, a young guy, only got four years, another seven. California was very, very soft on crime for a long time.

After two mistrials, I was sentenced to 12 years and 8 months. I was sent to Norwalk Reception Center first but I didn't last long there because I was deemed too dangerous for the environment. They then sent me to the Men's Central Jail in downtown Los Angeles where I was reprocessed. Because of the amount of extreme violence that I had piled up, they placed me into the gang module. This place was set aside for anyone in a gang in Los Angeles. If you had a reputation, a name on the street, that's where you were sent.

If you're a young gang member and put into this place, your shoulders are up, your chin is high and you think you're somebody. I wasn't in there to run things however, that's not how it goes down. A lot of schooling goes on in there. You're in with adult convicts and because LA County was so racially divided, I was not allowed in any way, shape or form, to talk to or communicate with black inmates. I could only talk to our group. That was our law. We only dealt among ourselves.

Our gang in jail was the Southern United Raza, or SUR. All the Southern California Hispanic gang members on the inside joined together and became one big gang. This was done not only for our protection but to organize crimes on the outside. The schooling was on such things as keeping your cell clean, learning a certain way to talk, who to hang with, and the chain of command. There's a whole lot of stuff you can and cannot do, you had to make sure that you abided by the rules. If you didn't follow the rules, your life could be taken in a moment. It was a very brutal environment.

I remember one man who was in there for doing a drive-by shooting where no one was killed. He got hit because he did the drive-by on someone he shouldn't have messed with. A bunch of members were assigned to hit him and he was stabbed to death. If you were in a dorm, they didn't have cells, you were with 120 guys and probably 119 of them were in there for murder.

It was a dirty time too, dirty from the standpoint of administration because the Sheriffs Department would put guys with outstanding tickets in our tanks. They did it for a reason. I can't imagine the fright when these people came in for petty crimes. Eventually this scandal came to light and the practice stopped.

I was housed in East Max, the unit was 2400. It was there I was selected to be a shot caller. I was responsible for holding every prison or jailhouse shank in there and was put in charge of distribution for anybody who needed a shank for a hit. I had authority, a big say-so on hits for anybody of whatever race who was out of line. That was a lot of power for a young man. I was just turning 18. Looking back as an adult, it was a time of either you or them and whatever had to be done to survive.

I was there in East Max for several months waiting to get bussed to my next destination. East Max had an immense amount of overcrowding at the time. The city of Los Angeles had over 3,000 gangs, they were all doing homicides, robberies and assaults and we were packed in like sardines.

Eventually I was transferred to North Kern State Prison in Delano, California, where I was held while being evaluated. The prison system scores you according to your crime, write ups, your behavior, your connections both inside and out and whether you're associated with a criminal enterprise or organized crime such as the Mexican Mafia.

I was given a high score, 97 out of 100, which meant I went straight to the SHU, the Solitary Housing Unit. It was an indefinite term while I awaited my next transfer. I was put into a single bunk, small cell, completely dark, a metal door and no windows whatsoever. I was in that cell all day, all night, for whatever time they decided. The Deputies decided your fate as to when you could come back out. They didn't tell me the amount of time I was going to be inside or when I could expect to get out. Eventually I knew I was going to get out, I had to, but there was no procedure for determining the time. It was left up to the guard's decision.

In that cell, I was fed the leftovers from the chow hall rolled into the form of meatballs. They were your breakfast, lunch and dinner. It was so dark, you couldn't see your hands but you could feel the plate and the juice, and the smell was like a dead rat. Nobody ate them. You didn't know which inmates handled them and for us Southerners we were told never to eat them.

After about 90 days of solitary at Kern, I was put on a bus headed for Sacramento. There were cages in the bus and if you are put in one of the cages, you were somebody: either a snitch, a rapist, a child molester or a shot caller. One of those four will get you put inside one of those cages. I was put into one for the long trip to California State Prison, New Folsom, Sacramento.

When I got there on November 7th, 1989, 6 days before my 19th birthday, I got off the bus, and what got my attention were the giant walls and a massive number of Correctional Officers, CO's, lined up in riot gear in front of the wall. That sight opened my eyes. I don't care how big, tough or street savvy I thought I was, when I saw those guys standing in front of me, something inside said, "Yeah, I really messed up. This is real."

The CO's got all the others off the bus first, then they got me. They escorted me to a room where the Warden and Gang Coordinator talked to me, and let me know personally that I would be spending my entire prison sentence in the SHU. I was a knucklehead who didn't care about their authority and I brushed off what they said because I didn't care.

I was then escorted to my cell where I would spend 23 hours of every day for the next years looking at walls. Strange as it is to admit now and as stupid as it sounds, I felt I had made it, I had a sense of pride that I was in this prison, that this is where the made gang members are, the shot callers are held here and I felt good about it.

Back then solitary confinement was solitary confinement. I was given white boxer shorts, a white tee shirt, a white sheet, a thin blanket and a roll of toilet paper. Visits were limited. I started my time.

I found out that once a month a Christian prison ministry from South Central LA, was allowed in on a Thursday. They bussed up. They would spend maybe 2 to 4 minutes each, talking to the guys in the cells. I wasn't looking for anything on the religious side but because of the small, contained pod we were in, I became familiar with every sound that was made and aware of every noise or movement that happened around me.

I was in for about 1 year and 9 months when this prison ministry came for a visit. A little black Christian lady who's name I later found out was Francis Proctor, was having a conversation with one of the CO's. She asked him, "Is that a cell down there?" She was asking about my cell but I didn't know at that moment she was asking about me. I was minding my own business but I could hear the conversation and the CO says to her, "Yeah, there is but you don't want nothing to do with that, nothing to do with that."

She was very bold. She wasn't taking no for an answer and the conversation went back and forth like on a ping-pong table and she keeps asking if she can approach my cell. The reason I know they're talking about me is I hear the CO say, "That's Diaz in there. You're wasting your time but go ahead and approach his cell." I heard her say to him, "You know Jesus came for everybody."

Next thing I know she's standing in front of my gate. Her first question to me was, "How are you doing?" I sarcastically said, "I couldn't be better." I got a chuckle out of her. She then said, "That was a stupid question."

I said, "It's all good." She said, "I want to invite you to a Bible Study here, I could sit with you..." and she starts selling me this religious thing and I'm not interested. I told her, "I'm cool with that, I want nothing to do with that, I'm ok." Again, she wasn't taking no for an answer.

She says to me, "I'm going to put you on my hit list." That was a colorful word that she used. She said again, "I'm going to put you on my hit list and Jesus is going to use you."

She said that and I thought to myself, "What is this lady talking about, she's lost her marbles. She doesn't know where she's at, she doesn't know who I am."

"Do you mind if when I come here I spend time with you? I want to pray for you," she said. I told her, "You can do whatever you want but I'm letting you know that I'm not interested in any of that religious stuff, that's not for me."

When she left that day, Francis Proctor began prayer intercession for a year and a half over my life. I really believe that it was her prayer and her obedience to her call to pray for me that brought me to a point where I had an encounter with Christ in my cell.

One day, I started to see what looks like a movie playing right there on my wall. I saw a mob of people surrounding a man carrying a cross. Nobody had ever told me the complete story of the crucifixion and what Jesus had to go through in order to save mankind. That wasn't on my radar.

This movie then starts playing everything I went through as far back as I could remember as a kid and it's all in order. As I watch this guy carrying a cross I know that whoever he is, he is looking at me. I can't see a face, but I know he's looking at me. And the movie goes from this footage to all the events that took place in my life as a gang member, as a leader both outside and inside prison. Every crime from stealing bicycles to home invasions to stabbings was in the movie.

And then I saw the nails going into his hands, his feet, I saw the cross being raised but here's the thing, I've been called Casey, a nickname I've had since childhood. I always hated my birth name, Darwin, since back in the days when I was a young kid and we were playing baseball and football. I just never liked it because in Los Angeles when I was in the gang I didn't want to be known as Darwin, come on, the name doesn't sound threatening. Not that Casey does either but there was just something about the name Darwin I didn't like. I told all the kids on my street that they were going to call me Casey and that name has stuck with me ever since. My folks call me that, uncles, aunts, everybody calls me Casey.

So I see this man on a cross, he's up there, hanging, I still can't see his face but he says to me, "Darwin, I did this for you."

When he said that, I could hear in that cell the very, very clear sound of someone losing their life, his breath left him. It was a familiar sound to me and at that moment I knew something had taken place not just in that cell, but really in my heart.

I remember kneeling, not knowing what I was doing but obviously repenting, getting real with God and asking Him to forgive me for stabbing this person, for this home invasion, for tying these people up, for shooting this guy. It was a real encounter with Christ. I remember weeping for what felt like hours, kneeling in the middle of my cell and feeling Godly remorse that set into my heart.

God spoke to me soon thereafter and I knocked on my gate to get the attention of the CO to ask for a Chaplain. I didn't even know what a Chaplain was. But I asked for one. The CO was really puzzled, he thought I was pulling his leg. It took some time but he brought me a form I filled out and gave back to him. Some days after, I found myself siting in a little room explaining to the Chaplain what took place, I see his bottom lip start to quiver, he starts shaking, tears are running down his face, and I cry because the whole thing I saw repeats itself.

He takes his Bible and starts reading about the walk to Golgotha, the walk that Jesus had to the cross and to his death. That moment really shook me to the core because that was exactly what I saw on that wall.

A short time after that conversation, God spoke to me again, letting me know that I was to call a gang meeting and to let them all know that I wanted nothing to do with them anymore, that I would tell them I was a Christian. To my mind, I thought that would be after I paroled out because I was supposed to be housed in the SHU for my entire sentence. There were no plans for me to ever get out of the SHU. But by a miracle, another God moment occurred.

The Warden and the Gang Coordinator came to my cell one day, opened the gate and told me I was being taken out of the SHU, I was going to be put into general population. This is exactly what I heard from God. They walked me into the mainline maximum security, level four yard. Lifers, murderers, gangs, you name it, they were all there.

It was made up in my heart that I was going to do this meeting. I got to the yard and as soon as I could, I let everybody know who was there, even shot callers from other gangs, that from that point on I wanted nothing to do with the gang, that I was now a Christian.

They all turned around, put their backs to me and walked away. I knew what that meant: a hit was going to be ordered on my life for stepping down.

In the Department of Corrections there are two laws: a convict law and prison politic law, and both say that if ever you step down, dissociate from a gang or go bad, your life is required. I knew the laws, and the requirement.

When it was going to happen, I was expecting more than one guy to come to my cell and finish the job. I would be lying if I said I wasn't afraid. I knew what was coming, my life was on the line. It was a long night. I waited and prayed. I knew most of the time hits were done in the morning when cell gates were racked open for breakfast.

I prayed and made a promise to God, which I don't recommend anyone does unless you're going to keep it, that I would never put my hands on anybody ever again. I wasn't going to make it difficult for them to do what needed to be done, stabbing me to death. In the morning I sat on the end of my bunk, I had my Bible in my left hand and I planned on not looking at them when they did it. I was just going to let them do what they needed to do, to kill me.

The gang shot callers assigned one of my very own gang members to do the hit. My gate cracked open in the morning and out of the corner of my eye I saw the guy come in, I saw the shank in his hand but I still didn't look at him. I thought there were going to be others with him to finish me off and it caught me by surprise that he was by himself.

He said to me, "You better be right because I can't do this. But I will roll with you."

That, I was not expecting. His name was Mosca, (fly in Spanish) and he turned to Christ right then and there. He became the first person I brought to the Lord. He had come into my cell with the full intention of not doing anything to me, not following through with the hit he was assigned, not killing me. He knew a hit would be placed on him for not doing the job. We would have hits placed on both of us.

Whatever happened to him in the hours prior to the time he stepped into my cell was between him and God. Something did happen to him but he wasn't aware of what was going on, or not going on. Again, this is the first guy I lead to the Lord and this was the guy who was ordered to do the hit, to kill me.

Mosca was known as a "good dude," a guy who followed the all the gang laws, an outstanding contributor to the organization and he was ordered to do the hit. Since a hit was ordered, he had no choice in the matter, he was compelled to follow through. In the past, he had no problem doing hits, doing what was required of him but there he was in front of me with a shank in his hand ready, but he couldn't do it.

After that, the two of us had to endure two years of brutal beatings. Countless numbers of times we ended up in the infirmary busted up badly. We would walk into the chow hall together and the next thing we knew, we had twenty to thirty South Siders on top of us beating the snot out of us. It was real anger they had towards us.

The sentence on me should have been carried out by Mosca but because it wasn't, both of our lives should have been taken. The question then became, "Why didn't they take our lives rather than just beat us?" The answer is because we were both Believers, God's hand was upon us in this whole deadly situation. In the gang's mind the thought was, "Let's not kill 'em, let's inflict as much pain as possible on them, make them suffer, let's have fun with these two for turning away from us."

A prison term for this kind of thinking is, "Hard Candy" and what that means is," Beat 'em almost to death." If a Shot Caller says, "We are going to put Hard Candy on homeboy," that means, "Beat 'em almost to death but don't kill 'em. Let's have fun."

For two years Mosca and I endured their fun. But in that time, we were able to use a system of communication to other inmates about our belief that everybody knew inside called 'kites'. Kites were small letters which passed information from institution to institution, inmate to inmate usually giving instructions on how to move drugs from outside to inside or to put hits on guys, again outside or inside. The system was carried on by us very carefully. I began to use kites to witness to some of the gang leaders.

I went for the top guns. I wrote these small letters, messages and questions and I handed them to these dudes. I knew that if they took the kites, I was certain they would read them. And little by little, one by one they started coming to Christ. One of the founders of MS-13 came to Christ through one of these kites. The message was usually a short scripture or a question such as, "Who are you trying to impress?" The messages were personalized to each individual because we were doing time together and I knew what each guy knew about all the moves that were going on, I knew about everything.

The kites were words of encouragement intended to make them think about their roles as adults or as young gang leaders. They were already in for life, others for double life, many were murderers, so I wrote telling them there was nothing else to prove to anybody. They had already committed the most heinous crimes they could commit while in a gang, so I asked them who were they trying to impress?

I wrote scriptures and little by little, one by one, they started to come to Christ. This was happening during the two years of Hard Candy. Within the first couple of months, there were maybe four of us, then five. It started small. We did Bible studies where we basically read the Bible in the King James Version. We didn't have the luxury of different translations so we had to get hip to the King James. The Holy Spirit lead us in truth and understanding.

We devoted ourselves to the reading and then we would talk about what we just read. Those were Bible studies to us, we didn't know what we were doing. I was writing kites with both scripture and words of encouragement, I was brutally honest with everybody and in the two years after my conversion, over 200 inmates in New Folsom State Prison came to know Christ.

I said earlier that usually if you make a promise to God, I recommend you don't break your word but unfortunately, that's what happened to me. I had told God I would not put my hands on anyone ever again but one day I was very disappointed because I was told a visit from my mom didn't pan out because of a paperwork problem. I hadn't seen my mom in years and it was one of those days in prison where you are looking forward to something nice happening in your life but it didn't happen. I was very disappointed and walking back to my pod with my Bible in my hand, a guy called me a "Bible Thumper."

I don't know what happened but I just snapped. I got in his face and said to him, "If you got anything to say or get off your shoulders, you're more than welcome to come inside my cell and we can take care of business."

My cell gate was cracked open, it wasn't open all the way, it was open just enough for him to stick his head in and he said to me, "We're going to take care of this in the chow hall."

I jumped off my bunk and snatched him inside the cell. I had my way with him. I had full intention to almost kill him and I remember grabbing his neck and his shirt and telling him, "If you ever give another Christian a hard time, if I ever see you doing anything to another Christian, the next time I'm going to make sure I kill you, I'm ending your life, I'm letting you know right now."

The beating was very brutal. When it was over, he wasn't coherent, he was like a rag doll, he had no idea where he was and I pushed him out of my cell. A lot of inmates saw this go down. I broke my vow to God.

I was washing my hands when one of the guards came by, I still had some of the guys blood on my face, I know the guard saw it, there's no way he didn't see it, he kind of looked at me like he knew what was up but he didn't say anything. He knew my life had been in danger, that I had endured beatings for two years but he just kept walking. I could have asked for lock up and avoided the beatings by asking for protective custody but I didn't. I was going to stay in there, in the middle of it all.

When a person is born again, you don't glow in the dark right away. Slowly, I had to deal with some of the issues inside of me, anger was one of them, it was a process with Christ and the Holy Spirit but God had a plan for me and used the beatings for His glory. Many men came to Christ during those two years, something good came from those beatings and that tough time.

I had been incarcerated for almost 9 nine years and I had taken college classes along with the court appointed classes that were mandatory: gang violence, gang awareness, victim awareness, and I had to attend AA and NA meetings. I was 25 years old and really didn't dig the last two meetings because, although my crime had nothing to do with drugs, I still had to take them.

For me, working on myself was staying disciplined, reading my Bible, spending hours and hours reading the Bible. If I was awake I read the Bible. There was no entertainment inside so the Bible was my thing and I was really OK with that. Growing up, my father didn't allow me to watch any sports on TV. He would throw books at me so the training of reading he gave to me, came to good use as I did the time.

I was required to complete the classes before getting out, there was no way that I couldn't take the classes and then show up before the parole board and expect release. I had to comply with the requirements and it was good for me to take the classes, I learned quite a lot. The staff brought victims of violent crimes into the classroom, they spoke to us about their experiences and what they had to endure. There were times when people spoke about losing a loved one to gang violence or being assaulted by a gang. They shared their stories so I learned about the victim's side of violence.

As a believer, I was made aware of how I had terrorized lives, how I really messed up people and how they wouldn't be the same person after the event because of my actions or the actions of other violent offenders. I learned things I wasn't aware of, or didn't care to be made aware of, before I was saved. Compassion became a part of me.

I came up for a parole hearing on July 3, 1995. I wasn't counting on getting out, I still had several years over my head and I thought I wouldn't be going home anytime soon. I was in the room with the board members and a Pastor stepped in. He caught me by surprise because he said to me, "I'm here to pray for you." I said to him, "You know I'm not going home, so what are we going to pray for?"

He said, "Well I'm here to support you, to pray for you."

We prayed together and I remember thinking how cool it was that this man took the time to make the drive and have the commitment to be there for me.

The hearing started and the usual questions from the panel came to me, "What have you been doing since the last time we saw you? What programs have you completed? How do you feel about your crime?" All of those.

Then they asked me a question they ask everybody; "Why do you think we should release you?"

I answered, "You shouldn't release me, I don't deserve to ever be out, in fact I deserve to be here for the rest of my life, I really do. The sentence the court imposed upon me was quite lenient. So I'm not looking forward to you releasing me, I need to serve out my time for the crime I'm in for. I take full responsibility for my actions. It's no one else's fault, it's mine, I made the choices and I don't deserve to ever be out. That's the truth."

We took a recess and when we came back they asked me, "What would you like for lunch?" I answered that I would like a hot meal. They then pushed paperwork in front of me. I read, "Parole granted." My jaw dropped, I couldn't believe it.

Not too long after the hearing I'm walking out the gate of the prison, exiting through Administration, the last door closed behind me and the only thing that is separating me from freedom are two Immigration Naturalization Agents standing in front of me. They asked me my name, even though they knew who I was and if I was born in El Salvador. I tell them Darwin Diaz and they tell me to put the box I was carrying down. They then chained me up, put me into the back of a small van and drove me to a Federal facility.

I thought that I was going to be deported to El Salvador, to the place where I was born. I didn't know anybody there, my Spanish wasn't all that good, I'm not your typical El Salvadoran, so I didn't know what was happening.

We arrived at the facility and they put me into a holding cell with a pay phone and two other guys, two Mexican nationals who speak little English but who have been transferred to this place from another prison. We started a conversation and they asked me where I was born, if I had family, kids, a wife? The guards asked if I wanted to make a phone call and I said no, I didn't want to call my mom and disappoint her, to break that lady's heart again.

I then started witnessing to these two dudes one by one, sharing my story. I tell them what took place in New Folsom. The first guy I talked to started to take heed to my words. Within minutes I lead him to the Lord.

In my release box that I brought from New Folsom, are two Spanish Bibles still in shrink wrap. I had never opened them, I can read a little Spanish, I'm not fluent in it but I kept them. For what? For this. They were in my box but the box was outside the holding tank.

I went up to the gate, to the bars as one of the Agents was walking by and I ask him if he could get me one of the Spanish Bibles from my box. He got one out of my box, gave it to me through the bars and I gave it to the dude I had just witnessed to. Now the second guy and I started talking and within minutes the three of us were holding hands and I lead him to the Lord.

Almost immediately after I lead the second guy to Christ, one of the INS Agents came to the gate and said to me, "We made a mistake. We can't release you from here. We are going to take you back to New Folsom." Go figure. I lead two guys to the Lord because of an administrative mistake!

I was returned to the prison and within 24 hours released again. I wanted ice cream more than anything else so I got some and because I was used to eating fast prison meals, I went to town on it and got the biggest brain freeze ever known to mankind. It was my first food outside and I can say it was quite an experience to look back and see God's hand upon my life, something I have a hard time explaining. God had mercy on me, I should have been dead but God gave me a second chance.

Darwin "Casey" Diaz has taken advantage of the second chance God so mercifully gave him. Soon after being paroled, Casey visited Francis Proctor's South Los Angeles Baptist Church during a Sunday service. The Church was packed and Francis Proctor and the prison ministry were all sitting in the front pews. A joyful, tearful, hugging reunion ensued with

Francis and her group in a very special moment. God had brought them together for the purpose of Francis seeing the fruits of her labor. When Casey was married, the ministry attended. Francis has since passed on.

Casey has written a very popular book entitled, "The Shot Caller," has had a documentary made of his life and is presently devoting his time to speaking engagements before at-risk-youths, colleges, Christian groups and churches. He speaks in prisons regularly and has recently been invited to speak inside 27 different prisons to tell the story of his life.

For more information on how you can partner with his ministry, visit Caseydiaz.net

5

"Drugs: The Devil's Communion"

"Look for yourself, and you will find in the long run only hatred, loneliness, despair, rage, ruin, and decay. But look for Christ and you will find Him, and with Him everything else thrown in." C.S Lewis

Brandon Boyce's witnessed his family collapse around him because of drug use and addictions. The downward spiral was responsible for two uncles and a brother dying and his parents divorcing. Drugs then led to homelessness, burglaries and panhandling with his father to support their mutual habit. Jail and prison followed. Fortunately, so did Jesus Christ.

BRANDON BOYCE
Death Or Prison podcast, Number 26.
8 years inside.

I was born July 12, 1982, grew up in Green Acres, Florida, and in the beginning had a really good household. I had a great father, a loving mother and an older brother. In that house, my dad tried to provide the best for us the only way he knew. He spoiled me. When Nintendo came out in 1986, he made sure I had one and every Christmas he always got me what I wanted, what I asked for. That's the kind of family I had. He was that kind of dad, so I was spoiled rotten as you might suppose.

Growing up I wanted to be like my dad, l looked up to him, I idolized him and wanted to be just like him. He was a State Champion Kickboxer in the 1970's and demanded respect from everyone who knew him. People gave the respect to him. Some people feared him. He ran his own construction company with about thirty men working under him. They all looked up to him so from that aspect, he was a good role model.

But on the other hand, he bought and sold drugs. I started smoking pot when I was nine. I picked my dad's roaches out of ashtrays, took them to the bathroom and smoked them. As time went by, I started to dabble, to use other drugs that were made available in the house. When I was thirteen I started smoking pot with my dad. He discovered that I was smoking and he made the decision to smoke with me. He felt that if I smoked at home, I was in a safe environment and that he could keep an eye on me. He didn't know I was doing other drugs.

At the age of fifteen, I was selling pot for my dad to the construction guys so drugs became very prevalent and very much a part of my life. When I was sixteen I started using cocaine. My brother would get some, bring it home and we did cocaine together. At nineteen I started using heroin. I lived in a house that was a very popular hangout, everyone came over because I had the newest stuff, the best toys so I always had friends over and we got drugs for them.

I had two uncles who were occasionally homeless and they stayed at our house when they had no other place to stay. My dad allowed them to spend the night sometimes so there would be six of us in the house and there would always be drugs. That was the environment I lived in.

I was very close with both of my uncles, we watched TV and ate peanuts together. Eventually this all turned bad when the youngest, my uncle Lenny, died from an overdose of heroin. I remember the day a Police Officer came to the house and told my dad that his younger brother had died and dad broke down and cried. I will remember that day for the rest of my life because he was crying and broken. From that point on, my dad went on a downward spiral. He used drugs to try and numb the pain and escape the reality he had to face. I realize now that I used drugs later in life for the same purpose.

Dad started looking at porn and he would get high, out of his mind. He stopped paying any real attention to what I was doing, he didn't realize I was using heavy drugs, cocaine and heroin.

My mom couldn't take it anymore and divorced my dad when I was eighteen. She knew my dad, my brother and I were all using. She was really traumatized by all of our behavior. We had been manipulating her the whole time, stealing from her. She finally decided she didn't want to be around us or to enable what we were doing anymore. The decision to divorce my dad and move out was really hard on her as you might expect. She didn't use drugs and to see her family, people whom she loved, destroying our lives really affected her.

She tried to help my brother and me and made a decision to get a place for us to live separately from my dad. She wanted us away from his influence. She got us a trailer and we lived together for some time. It was a bad environment for both of us because we got high all the time and used all the drugs we could get our hands on. My mom, after she got my brother and me the trailer, was totally out of the picture, she was gone. My dad had his own place, a trailer he had rented for himself. It got to the point where my brother and I and even dad, couldn't afford or manage our separate rents, so the three of us moved in together, we lived in one trailer.

All of our addictions progressed and got worse. My habit got so bad that I couldn't go to work or hold a job. I started stealing to get money. I stole some aluminum shutters from a porch, got arrested and was charged with burglary of an occupied dwelling. This was my first experience having to face hard prison time.

Prior to this charge, I had been arrested more than once beginning at the age of sixteen, for several drug charges. At sixteen, I was arrested for possession of half an ounce of weed and I was sentenced to complete community service. From time to time after that first arrest, I got arrested for possession. I did one forty-five day and one six month sentence in the County jail. I once got caught with some bags of heroin and did ninety days in County. Programs were offered in County to help guys like me but I didn't want any help, I didn't take any programs, all I wanted was to do the time, get back out and start using again.

When the trial for the burglary of the occupied dwelling ended, I was sentenced to one year and a day in prison. I did the time and when I was released, they gave me $100 and a train ticket. That same day, I went to the store and bought a six pack of Natural Ice and started drinking and there it went, my addiction spiraling again. I got into a halfway house, stayed there awhile but I left and went back to living with my dad and brother in 2008.

When I moved back in with them, I started using again, that's what I wanted. We lived for two years together and then in 2010, we all got evicted and found ourselves on the street. The three of us were homeless, living in a tent in the woods in West Palm Beach, Florida, and panhandling on street corners for small change, handouts. That was our existence.

I will never forget one really bad day. My dad, brother and I were holding cardboard signs at an intersection begging for money. I watched my dad. Here was a man who had been State Kick Boxing champion, who had once owned his own construction business, who had had a family and a house, he was a provider and as I watched him my anger grew and I blamed God for where we were. I asked myself, "How did we get here, how could God let this happen in our lives?" That was a real low point for me.

The panhandling went on for a while and then one day we heard about a church called Westgate Tabernacle. It was a church offering food and a bed for a night. We felt it was a chance to get off the street. The church had a requirement that if you were going to sleep and be fed, you had to attend church service for two hours. I remember I hated that I had to spend my time in a service, and I hated my life because I was going through withdrawals most of the time I was in church. When I wasn't going through withdrawals, I was getting high in the church bathrooms and nodding off during services. They eventually found out what I was doing and kicked me out of the church. I was banned.

My dad and brother were upset because it was either church or sleeping on a canal bank with the mosquitos and all the other bugs. I was out there by myself and they felt badly for me so they eventually left the church for me.

The only way I could support my addiction was to start stealing again. I ended up getting arrested on thirty-one felony charges, nine different cases of stealing copper and other construction material.

After I was locked up and in jail facing all of those charges, the authorities told me I was looking at five years. They were going to put me away because I had priors, one of which was the burglary of an occupied dwelling. It was then that I asked God to get me out of this. I pursued Him because I wanted Him to get me out of the circumstances I got myself into.

While I was in the jail waiting trial, in my mind I kept hearing songs that were sung in Westgate Tabernacle Church. They flooded my mind, the words kept coming back to me. Songs like, "Open The Eyes of My Heart," and a song by Casting Crowns, "East To West." The song talked about our sins being cast by God as far as the East is from the West. They were the songs that I had sung and God was using the words to draw me back to Him.

I appeared in Court before Judge Rap. Everybody in jail told me when you get before Judge Rap, it's a 'wrap.' He sentenced me to five years. I was upset, angry because God didn't come through for me as I hoped and prayed He would. He didn't get me out of the mess I had made, He didn't rescue me as I had asked Him.

I was first sent to South Florida Reception Center, then transferred to Moore Haven Correctional Facility. When I got there, I pushed the Bible away, I pushed going to Chapel away, I pushed God away, I didn't want to do anything spiritually. I did the time and this feeling lasted, it persisted. I was also assigned to Henry Work Camp. As my release date neared for the end of my five-year sentence, I was transferred to Sago Palm Reentry.

On July 11, 2012, the first day I got to Sago Palm I got high, drugs and weed were readily available. But this day turned out to be a very significant day in my life. When I got to my dorm, all my roommates were getting high and smoking what we called K2. They were passing it around so I ended up getting high, sitting on my bunk with my headsets on and a Bible in front of me. The Bible was a way to block out the world, to tell my roommate, the Officers and everybody else, "Leave me alone, I'm in my own world."

So, I've got my Bible open, my headsets on, I'm smoking and getting high, I wasn't reading anything but I was listening to WAY FM. Looking back on that time, I am so thankful today that I was listening because a song was played at that very moment which changed my life, "White Flag" by Chris Tomlin. The song talks about waving our white flags, about surrendering all. It talks about a battle that rages in our rebel heart and the fight we cannot win, we surrender, said the lyrics. Through that song, God began to speak to me. Again. This time I listened.

My thoughts became that I couldn't leave prison in the condition I was in. I had one foot inside and one foot outside, one foot in the world and the other trying to pursue God. I was on the fence and I knew that I needed to surrender my life completely to God if I wanted to change. I knew I had to make a choice, that I was going to either choose the ways of God and the Word of God, or I was going to continue to do what I had been doing.

So, on that day, July 11, 2012, I made the decision to surrender and I told God that no matter what I was to face, I was going to pursue Him wholeheartedly. I told Him that I was going to seek Him every day, regardless of the opposition or the failure, I was going to persevere.

When I made that decision, my whole life began to change. The change didn't mean that I didn't have sin in my life, it didn't mean that I had no more failure in my life, but that I was able to get back up when I did fall and continue forward. I was being real about my life and I was being real with God. He began to change my heart, my thinking and I started to get involved in the church prison, the Chapel, little by little.

The Chapel needed someone to lead worship, there was only one guy who would get up and lead. I was always in front singing because once I surrendered, once I was saved, I couldn't help but sing in Chapel or wherever I was. I was driving everyone in the dorm crazy. God put a song in my heart so I volunteered to help lead worship with another brother.

Then one day someone asked if anyone wanted to preach. It ended up being a competition with some of the guys preaching the message, others listening. This was something good in my life. I volunteered to preach and the first message I gave, I will never forget. It was about "My Father's Business," the story of Jesus getting left behind in the Temple by his mother and father. They find him and he says to them, "Don't you know I must be about my Father's business?" I will always remember that message because now I always want to be about my Father's business.

My mom didn't know about my transition. When I was in jail or prison, even though she had mostly left the picture, she always wrote to me. I was able to call her once every two weeks or so during that time. But because of my change, my relationship with her got better. Because of my experience and the change she witnessed in me, she started looking into the word of God. She began a class on Proverbs and our relationship blossomed. She knew I was a Believer and then eventually, my dad and brother knew from the letters I wrote them. They all realized that I had changed.

But life is never without low points. Five months before I was released from Sago Palm, March of 2014, I got a call out to come down to classification. The Officer handed me the phone and told me it was my mother and when I picked it up, she was crying profusely. At this point I'm thinking of my dad because he had been going steadily down the dark road of drugs the whole time I was away. But mom told me that my brother had passed away, he had overdosed on heroin. I was numb at this point and the only thing I could tell her was what immediately came to my mind; Proverbs 3:5, "Trust in the Lord with all your heart. Lean not on your own understanding but acknowledge him in all your ways and He will direct your path." I spoke those words to her because I believed them and I trusted the Lord.

Before my brother passed away, I had lost two uncles from drug addiction and my dad had had a stroke in 2013. He had a seizure while he was getting high. He lost all of his motor skills and afterward with therapy, he had to learn to walk and talk again. He is still alive today. When I have conversations with him, he blames himself for everything. He was the older brother, the husband, the father, the dad, he was the one who had the big influence on all of our lives.

Because I had surrendered my life to Jesus, I thought naively that everything was going to be great from then on. That is not life, though, life is full of trials and heartache. It's a process. When I look back on my life, I see how God was always there for me, trying to get me to turn to Him, trying to get my attention. Finally, that one day, July 11, 2012, in Sago Palm Reentry, the whole thing finally clicked, I started to see things clearly, the old man was gone and the new man showed up. It was the turning point in my life. From that day forward, I was a work in progress, working out my salvation, allowing God to saturate my heart and mind. As He worked on me each day, God began to set me apart, to sanctify and cleanse me from the inside out. I had to learn His ways and let go of other ways I had learned in my life.

The guys around me weren't sure about my commitment. One time I was on the recreation yard praying with two other guys and a guy walks by and says to us, "You guys are all crackheads, you'll always be crackheads." The devil is a liar and I prayed for him. There was another guy who I had grown up with, a childhood friend, who saw what was going on in my life and who criticized me saying, "Man, you're always on that Jesus stuff," because I was ministering to him every chance I got. But before he was released, he came to my dorm and asked me to pray for him. He was getting ready to go back out, he knew what I stood for, what I represented and he sought me for prayer. I was honored in that moment.

I was released from Sago Palm Reentry in August 2014. This is where you see the victory in my life. I got connected with Kirk's Prison Ministry, a group of men who visited prisons and I knew them from their visits. I was at work release and I called one of them and asked for a job. They told me I could work part time in a warehouse for Regal Paint and Decorating, a Benjamin Moore dealer. Something transpired over time and their warehouse manager had to be let go. Guess what, I was next in line for the job because I had worked beside him.

I then had an income and not long after getting work, I get an apartment offered me by Anchor House, a transition home for guys just out of prison. I stayed there two years and saved money for my own place. I became an usher in a church called Common Grounds and I got heavily involved with the church's activities. I stayed in touch with Kirk's Ministry and after two years, I was allowed to go back into prisons and preach and give my testimony every third Sunday at the same prison where I was incarcerated, in the same Chapel room where I had first preached and where I had led worship.

God has been so good to me. I have a beautiful wife and family and they see Christ in me. I want to say to everyone reading this that what has been done in my life can be done in yours. My life was bound, chained to addiction and drugs but I was set free, liberated because all things are possible through Christ Jesus. God can liberate you and show you what it is to be a man or woman of God and to walk in virtue and integrity. You really can live a life of purpose and be an inspiration to those around you.

For the past three years, Brandon has worked full time for Prison Fellowship as Prison Ministry Manager. He is a dedicated man working with love to increase the size of God's Kingdom. He has been sober for 12 years. Keep up the God Work Brandon!

Kenneth C. McKenzie

6

"Don't Play With God"

"It is good for me that I was afflicted, that I might learn thy statutes." (Psalm 119:71)

"One of my favorite verses from my favorite Psalm." Dietrich Bonhoeffer

Adam Jolly was self admittedly, a menace to society for much of his life. Looking at how he was raised, he didn't have much of a chance to be otherwise. But while he was incarcerated, salvation happened in a moment. Today, Pastor Adam Jolly and I end our conversations with, "I love you man." And we mean it.

PASTOR ADAM JOLLY
Death Or Prison podcast Numbers 55, 58, 59.
28 years inside.

I was born a handsome little fellow on September 11, 1964, in Belle Glade, Florida. My mom and dad decided to have me raised by my great grandmother, Ma Jennie, who lived in Stuart, Florida, about one hour's drive from Belle Glade. Ma Jennie was about 6'3," and had a backhand everyone respected. I was dropped off by my parents at her house before I started kindergarten.

There were twelve of us in Ma Jennie's house; Ma Jennie, my two brothers, seven uncles, one aunt, and me. Two of my uncles had served in Vietnam. Another uncle was selling drugs and pimping women.

At a very early age I watched and absorbed the lifestyle of those around me. I learned about the sale and use of both marijuana and crack cocaine.

Triple X porn movies were also on in the house so I learned a lot about the raw side of life beginning around the age of eleven.

It was a normal, everyday scene that people came to our house to buy marijuana or crack cocaine from our family. It was a lifestyle, something acceptable for our four generations to be selling drugs to the neighborhood, including Ma Jennie, my grandmother, my mother from her home in Belle Glade and my brothers and uncles in Ma Jennie's house. Each day I saw all this drug selling and money making happening before my eyes. I felt that what my family was doing, I was supposed to do. They were living examples of how I was to plan and live my life.

I couldn't wait to go to school then come home to watch everybody sell drugs. I went from shooting marbles in the sixth grade to getting an education in selling Mary J in the seventh grade.

There was also a hardness in my heart toward my parents because they weren't raising me and I didn't know how to process that fact because we didn't talk about it. We just kept moving forward, nobody complaining.

I look back now and realize how my life was determined by what some call a generational curse. My great grandparents were living it, my grandparents were living it, my mom and dad lived it and I was in the middle of living it. It's a curse because everything done in life as an unbeliever is a tough pattern to break. There were times I wanted to break from it, but it is something inherited, something very powerful that more often than not, will influence people to do wrong before they do right.

Visiting my parents in Belle Glade one weekend in 1978 when I was thirteen years old, I devised a master plan on how to come up with fast money. It was in Belle Glade when I first heard the song, "For the Love of Money," by the OJ's and I was inspired. I saw men and women selling drugs and doing prostitution on street corners where the love of money was something serious.

The environment was right for my plan and I started the hustle. Things moved a lot faster in Belle Glade than in Stuart, so I worked on making connections with the right people to get Mary J. on a large scale and at a low price. My plan was to sell weed at my school in Stuart.

I returned to Stuart excited by the idea. I now knew where to get Mary J, how to sack it, how to distribute it, but most importantly how to get paid after the sale. I wasn't going to be a broke player. The whole idea was an appealing, attractive life, normal for my Stuart family so it was normal for me and I fell right into it. I started selling weed to kids at middle school. I had a target audience. I started smoking it as well.

I was in the seventh grade, thirteen years old, selling weed, when I had my first encounter with law enforcement. Just when business was booming and things were going smoothly, I was told one day to report to the principal's office. I made sure I was clean and straight but all sorts of things raced through my mind. I assured myself that whatever the problem was I had to be cool and not let them see me sweat.

The first faces I saw were the three white guys I called, Larry, Curly and Moe. I had sold three sacks of weed to them earlier in the day. They were still high. Their faces were totally red, they had glossy eyes and they all were shaking like Rodney Dangerfield. The next two faces I saw were two Sheriff's Officers who were wearing looks that indicated I was in serious trouble.

I saw the principal, Mr. Don Wallen, sitting behind his desk with a look of disbelief on his face. He was a highly respected man. On his desk were two of the sacks I had sold these clowns. Mr. Wallen expressed his disappointment with me because on many occasions he had taken the time to speak to me as a father would his own son. He told me once that greatness was down inside of me, that I had a unique talent to do something special with my life. His talk didn't resonate.

I fessed up and took responsibility for my actions. I was cuffed, put into the back of a Sheriff's car, transported and booked into my first incarceration at the Detention Center in Ft. Pierce.

Before all of this went down, Ma Jennie had taken me to visit two uncles who were in Florida prisons. They were in for robbery, kidnapping, selling drugs and battery on law enforcement officers. Visiting them with Ma Jennie, the prison never struck me as a bad place to be. Although it wasn't my dream or desire to do time, the visits numbed me to the fear of being locked up.

So I wasn't too afraid when I was put into a one-man cell at the Juvenile Detention Center. To my surprise, church services were offered and I attended. I heard some familiar words and people I didn't know prayed with me. Living with Ma Jennie, as strange as it sounds, church was mandatory for all us kids. She tried to teach us a reverence for God and to develop a respect for His word, but we weren't willing to surrender our rebellious ways. Jesus was a Sunday kind of thing. I can still hear her prayers today: "Lord, don't let the Devil kill my boys."

Ma Jennie was my only visitor at the Detention Center and I served twenty one days. She picked me up and put me back in school soon thereafter where I was labeled a troublemaker and a bad influence. Kids were warned by their parents to stay away from me.

I temporally learned from my mistake. I tried to modify my behavior, to better myself, but I was living with and under the influence of a great grandmother who was seventy years old, a great grandfather, many other siblings, and family members. Ma Jennie tried to raise me the best way she could but with all of her effort and church going combined with the home lifestyle, she couldn't teach me to be a responsible young man and stay out of trouble. There were just too many influences in the opposite direction.

I visited my mom's house in Belle Glade most every weekend. My mom and dad were now separated so she lived alone. She was about one hour away from Stuart and on one visit, I told her that if I didn't get back to living with her in Belle Glade, I was going to rob everybody in Stuart who was white. That's the way I felt. That was my threat. On the weekend before I was to start my freshman year at Martin County High School, I convinced my mother to allow me to finish my education at Belle Glade High School. But I was Ma Jennie's baby boy and she didn't want me to leave her so she set up a contract between all of us: I had to finish my freshman year at Martin County High School, attend church with her, get a job and stay out of trouble. After I had fulfilled the contract, then and only then could I live in Belle Glade with my mom.

Immediately I started to work on my part of the bargain. I got a job and attended church every Sunday to hear the Gospel preached. The services were always uplifting as one of the mothers of the church, Mrs. Willie Mae Johnson, would jump up and down and shout, "Hallelujah!" Another church mother, Mrs. Janie Mae, would always have kind, encouraging words for me. These wonderful women were always telling me that God had a plan and a purpose for my life and that they saw something special in me. I didn't know what they were talking about.

One year passed and I thought Ma Jennie had forgotten our agreement, but my mom showed up at the end of the year ready to take me home. Ma Jennie was happy for me but at the same time her heart was sad that her baby boy was leaving. Understand that in Belle Glade, there is a bar on every corner, one playing music of the OJ's, another playing James Brown or Teddy Pendergrass. When I returned there with my mother, I saw everybody getting money selling 'heavy' drugs and that got me thinking on a whole different level. I started dipping and dabbing with cocaine, both selling and using it at the same time I was in Belle Glade High School. But this scene didn't last long. Just before my senior year I got arrested again for selling drugs.

This time I was incarcerated at the West Palm Beach Detention Center until I was committed to the Okeechobee Boys Home. I turned seventeen inside while serving a ninety-day sentence.

Things escalated to a whole new level after I got out. My uncle Mickey, a Vietnam vet, asked me one day if I wanted to make some serious money. He said it would take some traveling. I was all in, no matter the scenario or the consequences. When it came time to leave, Mickey and his girlfriend Bonnie, picked me up at Ma Jennie's. We were going north to Tallahassee and Panama City. Mickey had some unfinished, cash business there. He came into the house to get me and Ma Jennie saw us leaving. She had a word of prophecy for us. "If y'all get into that car, something bad is going to happen." I numbed my mind to her words and got into the car. I should have listened.

First off, we almost got killed driving up there. I fell asleep at the wheel driving seventy miles an hour, high on Mary J and I woke up to Bonnie screaming, Mickey yelling and the car spinning in circles on a wet highway. Only by the grace of God were we not hit by other vehicles. After we got turned around and headed north again, Bonnie begged and pleaded with Mickey to return home but Mickey being the Vietnam vet that he was, wasn't having any of it. His plan was that when we did head home, we were going to be carrying some major cash.

We arrived in Tallahassee and were met by Mickey's partner, Harry. He had two grocery bags full of twenties, fifties, and hundreds with him. Mickey knew there was more cash out there but we had to go to Panama City and rob some dudes to get it. Harry tried to get Mickey to leave with the cash in the bags but again, Mickey wasn't having any of the talk, he wanted more. His mind was made up.

We drove to Panama City in two separate cars. Diamond, Harry's wife was with him in the other car. We checked into two separate hotel rooms on the beach. Mickey, Harry and I then left to rob the dudes Mickey knew had some major money.

Six hours later, after the three of us committed the robbery, Ma Jennie's words came back to haunt me. Things started to fall apart. Harry and I were trailing Mickey miles away from the place where we committed the crime when Mickey was stopped for a routine traffic check.

Mickey, stupidly, was driving without a valid driver's license so he gets hauled off to the Panama City Jail where the police connect him to the stick up. Meanwhile, Harry and I drove away and checked into a Travelodge motel with more money than we could count. Harry then decided to walk to a McDonald's down the street because he was hungry. I stayed in the motel room.

I'm not sure how it happened but Harry got picked up by the police and thrown into the Panama City jail with Mickey.

I was counting the money about thirty minutes after Harry left when the phone rang. I was hesitant to answer but I did. I heard Harry say, "Don't say a word, just listen. I am in jail with Mickey and because I had the motel room key in my pocket, the police know where you are so get out of there right now. Leave town." I left the room with the cash. Minutes later I watched from a wooded area next to the motel as the police swarmed the area looking for me.

Sometime later I was trying to make a phone call to Bonnie and Diamond at their motel when police cars with lights and sirens descended on me. The police got out of their cars with guns drawn, threatening to shoot me if I moved. They directed me out of the phone booth and put a shotgun to my head. I kept saying to myself, "Lord don't let this fool pull the trigger!" They put me face down on the ground, cuffed me and transported me to the jail where Mickey and Harry were located. We were charged with three armed robberies in Panama City and four in Tallahassee. We also became suspects in every unsolved robbery from Ocala to Panama City.

When I turned eighteen on September 11th, some days later, I was adjudicated as an adult. Thirteen months after that, I was sentenced to four years to run concurrently with a twenty-five-year sentence I previously received in another courtroom in Panama City. Mickey got one life sentence and Harry got three life sentences. I didn't feel so bad after hearing those times.

The day arrived for me to leave for Sumter Correctional Institution, Florida, where I was to serve my time. Mickey told me to make a "weapon of destruction," a knife, to protect myself and if there came a time, not hesitate to use it. He told me that prison life wasn't based upon sympathy but that only the swift, wise, shrewd and strong survived in such a ruthless environment. We hugged after he gave me those words and then I hit him with a hard right cross to his chest for the twenty-five years I got for following him. Ma Jennie was sure right.

Sumter Correctional Institution was known by inmates as, "Gladiator School," because of the constant violence and senseless deaths that happened there. Doing my time, the name proved out right. I was involved in fist fights, knife fights, compound riots, and general senseless violence. During one of the riots, I got a fractured jaw and broken ribs. I almost lost my life.

In 1986, along with 215 other men, I was transferred to an even more deadly place, Martin Correctional Institution. The dark reality was that this place was a death trap for any man who failed to adhere to the convict code or who didn't play by the treacherous rules of the place. It was truly another planet on this planet. Daily busloads from other prisons dumped their load of violent men, walking time bombs ready to explode, convicts skilled in hurting and killing people. Most of these men had no regard for life whatsoever. They didn't discriminate on putting hurt on the blind, crippled, handicapped or crazy. They showed no remorse or conscience. In their world the strong survived by ruling the weak. A different set of demons lived at Martin in the hearts of men. I am talking demons of extortion, lasciviousness, homosexuality, rape, robbery, suicide, and murder. It was only by God's grace that I survived.

I knew that if ever I was going to get out and make a new life, I needed to get my GED and some vocational licenses. I studied and got my Air Conditioner and Architectural Drafting licenses. Only because of God, another inmate, a jailhouse paralegal with gifted skills, took an interest in my case, filed some appeals on my behalf and in October 1986, I received a court order for resentencing. When the smoke cleared, the judge gave me time served and fifteen years probation. I was released after four years from the hell and I walked out in 1987.

When I reported to my probation officer, he wanted to know my plan for staying out of prison and how I was going to survive in a drug-infested neighborhood, living with a drug dealing, dysfunctional family. He basically was telling me I had no chance to stay out long.

I tried going to church with Ma Jennie, joining the choir, even going to Bible studies but I was going through the motions without making a commitment to the Lord. I did this all in the name of religion. The Pastor during one of the services pointed his finger at me, and said, "God said He is calling you, and if you don't repent and receive Jesus, you are going to HELL!" The words convicted and scared me for a time but unknown to the Pastor, he had given me license and an excuse to drift away from the church.

When you are in prison, you get to know people who know people. So back in my element on the streets I started to roll with some of those contacts, selling what I could sell and getting the money for what I thought I needed. I was twenty-two years old and living the life. It takes money to be a player. I had a Mercedes Benz, jet skis, Rolex watches, all kinds of toys and I was working it.

Then I got busted again in November 1988, for trafficking crack cocaine. I hired Nelson Bailey, F. Lee Bailey's brother, to defend me and I was sentenced to a year and a day. This was my third incarceration and I did the time in Henry C.I.

In this season of my life, I couldn't explain it then, but a force was driving me, influencing my thoughts and actions and it wasn't a good force. I believed that I was really living but in truth I was chasing a deceptive mirage. My life was wasting away physically and I was dying spiritually. I thought I was balling but the sad reality was that I was falling.

During the years that I was out and running around, I was very promiscuous, having many relationships with different women and I wound up having seven kids, four girls and three boys. Because I never had a real role model in my life I had no idea how to be a father, a dad to my kids. I didn't know what being a dad was supposed to look like. Remember that my great-grandparents raised me. Everybody in my family was selling drugs so life was all about making money, taking care of the kids with the money and keeping it all moving forward.

I did my time for trafficking and in 1990, I was released from Henry C.I. Though I was a practicing sinner, I tithed to a local church and gave decent offerings to other churches. I believed in my heart that I was paying God off. I wore a big gold cross on a gold Gucci chain around my neck. I also helped some families with their finances by giving them money. I assisted community activists and donated my time riding disabled kids around on my jet skis. None of my good deeds, tithes, or offerings however, could stop the inevitable from happening.

On January 31, 1992, I was arrested for selling crack cocaine along with twenty-one other men in an undercover sting operation. While I was in the Martin County Jail, Ma Jennie was diagnosed with Alzheimer's disease and her mind started to deteriorate. That wasn't good news.

Thirteen months after I was arrested I was found guilty of selling and trafficking cocaine. The very moment the word "Guilty" was announced, I heard God's quiet voice in my heart clearly for the first time in my life saying, "You can't put any man before Me." The verdict crushed my family and friends who were in the audience. I was sentenced to fifty years as an habitual offender.

Living a thug's life had finally caught up to me, causing me to lose my freedom at great cost. What really pained me most though, was having to leave my kids without the ability to be their father. Before I was transported to Madison C.I., the authorities allowed me to see my kids. The time with them brought tears to my eyes.

I arrived at Madison C.I. in May of 1993, unchanged and still with the same criminal thinking and behavior traits I had learned on the outside. I began the hustle and flow of the game inside, I was smoking Mary J and doing drug sales, making money, but I began to feel disgusted and weary of the predicament I had put myself in. One year into my sentence Ma Jennie died. Her death saddened me greatly. It wasn't long after her passing that I started to attend church services. I sensed for the first time, an urgent need to be saved.

My cousin Mike had gotten saved in prison, released after his time was up and came to visit me. His conversation was Christ centered which was strange coming from him, but I listened to what he had to say about salvation. Before he left that day, he prayed for me to have my own personal experience with Jesus Christ.

Shortly thereafter a Christian inmate began witnessing to me about Jesus Christ every time he saw me. I tried to intimidate him with a prison tactic he was familiar with, but he looked me right in the eyes and said boldly, "What's in me is greater and more powerful than what is in you!" I didn't understand his words but I felt a force behind what he said. I couldn't shake this Christian off of my tail so to get him to leave me alone, I agreed to listen to a preacher on the radio named Tony Evans. Not only did this preacher make sense teaching the word of God, but he sounded like Richard Pryor.

After we listened together to Tony Evans, this Christian inmate shared two things with me that I will never forget. First, he said, "You are in the wrong army." Second, "When you surrender your life to Jesus Christ you are going to be a force to be reckoned with because you are going to be a five star general in God's Kingdom."

I was still slack after that talk and even during an altar call in Chapel, I didn't respond and hardened my heart. It was soon after that, that an inmate had to airlifted out of Madison due to a serious head injury. A dime was dropped on me and an anonymous lie fingered me as the perpetrator. I was removed from the open compound and placed into Administrative Confinement (AC) along with several other inmates who were associated with me, pending an investigation.

A Classification Officer came to see me in AC to tell me that the Administration was out to nail me. As I entertained my limited options, I concluded my back was against the wall and I had no way out of this jam. That day after the count, a fishing line was thrown perfectly under my locked cell door from another cell. At the end of the line was a lit stick of Mary J.

Once I hit on it and was under its influence, I found myself trying to cut a deal with God. I told Him that if He got me out of this jam I would serve Him with all my heart. Not realizing who I was talking to or what I was saying or committing to, almost in the same sentence I told God that I wasn't ready to surrender my life completely to Him, not just yet, and I asked Him to give me a little more time to handle my business. I was bargaining. You don't play with God.

The very next thing I knew I was on my knees in my cell telling God how disgusted I was with my life and that I was sorry for the way I was living. I opened a Bible I had while I was still on my knees and began to read a verse I had never seen before: "If you confess with your mouth, Jesus is Lord, and believe in your heart that God has raised Him from the dead, you will be saved," Romans 10:9. Immediately after reading, believing and confessing this scripture, something happened inside me. I stood to my feet and I felt the weight of my burdens had been lifted off of me. The feelings of guilt and shame were gone.

As my Mary J high evaporated, I felt a real peace. Joy had been released into the empty void of my soul. The reality was that I had genuinely accepted Jesus Christ into my heart to be my personal Lord and Savior based upon the authority of God's word in 2 Peter 3:9, "The Lord is not slack concerning His promise, as some count slackness, but is long suffering toward us, not willing that any should perish but that all should come to repentance."

This life changing experience took place on November 17, 1996, after I was in for five years. From that day forward, I lost the desire to smoke Mary J and the desire to hustle drugs. I was done with the hustle and the game. I went from a sinner to a saint overnight. With a clean heart and mind I told God whatever His will was for my life, I would do it. At that moment, when I accepted Jesus into my life, my mentality changed completely. I was reborn and transformed.

Understand that living in prison in the Florida Department of Corrections, it's a society within a society. The strong prey on the weak as I've said and, in some institutions, it's kill or be killed. It's that simple. You can be minding your own business and you look where you shouldn't or you walk into some place where you're not supposed to be, you do something wrong according to the convict code and your life could be taken in an instant. Lifers, men who will never get out and who have little to lose, rule.

Prison is a place where you have to prove yourself, where you have to earn your stripes. It's not a nice place. You have to fight for your manhood. If you don't stand up for yourself, many things can happen not the least of which is being forced into having sex with another man. Those men in prison reading this know exactly what I'm saying.

When I accepted Jesus though, everybody knew I was for real by my actions. I walked the talk. There are those in prison who say they are saved but they really never had the special encounter with God, the one that counts. I had that real encounter and He changed my life, gave me a new heart and a new spirit. I started to walk by faith. But I was still going to be tested.

I was transferred back to Martin C.I. and because of my faith, my confession of Jesus Christ, my life was threatened three times, two times with a knife. God stopped one guy who was going to stick me, literally right in front of me.

Leaders of the Crips, Bloods, Skinheads, the Devil worshippers, these real killers, respected me. They told me, "Hey Jolly, you're our preacher." They saw me going through this transformation. Living my life day in, day out, week in, week out, I established my reputation. I remained faithful to Him as He was to me. After some time, I started preaching to about 750 inmates every week, no matter if it was raining, thirty five degrees or one hundred degrees, I preached the Gospel of Jesus Christ the last seventeen years of my sentence on a hill in the Martin C.I. compound.

When I got saved, my daily prayer every morning, every night from my cell was, "God, cut my kids a little of the blood of Jesus," and He did that. Along with preaching, I started to be a father from prison. I wrote letters, I made phone calls to them. Visitations were important, they would ask me what I was going to do once I was out. First, I had to get out and then prove to them that I wasn't going back. I told them that not going back was the message. In all these ways I was planting important seeds. Why were they important? Three things: Because I was saved, because I gave God my word and because I intended to live out what my kids wanted from me.

So today all of my kids are adults and none of them use drugs. I Thank God. All have jobs. They are living on their own. They have educations and I am proud of them. All those factors are major blessings. I have made amends with their mothers and their grandmothers. I told all of them I was wrong, that I was sorry for all the drugs and I asked them for forgiveness and apologized for all the lies I told. I told them I was going to take care of my kids and I meant what I said.

To all the men behind the walls, write those letters to your kids, start being a father right now from where you are. Pray for your children, even if they don't respond, don't give up, stay faithful. For all those years I was inside, I missed birthdays, graduations, baseball games, soccer games, I can't make up for that lost time, I can't make up for what happened in the past. But more importantly, God helped me change where my future was going with my kids. Men reading this can use the same plan inside and out.

I served twenty two years of my fifty year sentence, the last seventeen years teaching the Bible on the compound. God blessed me out. When I was released I was put on eight years probation. I used that time to obtain a Doctorate in Divinity and Theology and a Master's Degree in Christian Counseling from Jacksonville Theology Seminary.

Pastor Adam Jolly is the founder and president of Fishers of Men Kingdom Outreach Ministry. Weekly, he shares the Good News of the Gospel inside Florida's prisons and jails, visiting the institutions where he was once incarcerated. Pastor Jolly represents as Coordinator, the Jack Brewer Foundation's Fatherhood Initiative Program, a ministry designed to shine God's light on the importance of being a father to men who are incarcerated. Love Ya Man!

Kenneth C. McKenzie

7

"Monster Man and an Angel's Face"

"To understand all is to forgive all." Baruch Spinoza

This is not an easy story to read. In Spinoza's words, there is a lot to forgive in Alonzo Dixon's life. I have included Alonzo's testimony, as gut wrenching as it is, because I want the reader to understand there are two important parts to the story and to his life: 1) evidence of the depth of evil to which Alonzo sank; 2) more importantly, the reality that there is no pit, no black hole, no evil so great, that God can't through His love, reach down, pull a person out and lead that individual to a life of transformation and redemption. (Romans 8:37-39)

Alonzo's parents divorced when he was very young. Soon thereafter, his mother moved his family from Texas to South Central, Los Angeles. South Central is known for being a rough place to raise a family, especially difficult for a single mom. Alonzo learned quickly what the streets teach many: survival in its rawest terms. In his own words he was an evil man. He sank into a 'sinkhole' of degradation, but for God…

ALONZO DIXON
Death Or Prison podcast, Numbers 97, 98, 99.
30 years inside.

I was born on an Army base in San Antonio, Texas, in 1963. When I was five my mom and dad divorced and mom took five of us kids, one older brother, older sister, one younger brother, younger sister and me and moved to South Central, Los Angeles. Unfortunately both of my brothers were eventually killed because of gang violence. Many people don't understand that this area of the world was, and still is, a neighborhood where there are two types of people: sheep and wolves. I learned quickly that I didn't want to be a sheep so I became a wolf. It was my means of survival. I was a product of my environment.

I want to be honest. Where I grew up, it was rape, robbery, murder and death on a daily basis. That's just the way life was for us. I became immune to feelings because there were so many emotions to deal with. Bullets were flying everyday, police were constantly around because of beatings, stabbings or shootings. I tuned all of it out and got to the point where nothing bothered me. And I think that is where Satan really, really took hold of me because human life, by the time I was twelve years old, meant nothing to me. It was my thinking and the way my life was: I either fit in or I didn't, I had to get out of the way or I would get run over. I didn't want to get run over.

My mom did the best she could to raise five kids but food was scarce. I wanted to help put food on the table but my method of helping put more stress on her. At twelve years old I began to rob people. I stole bikes and would ride them to white neighborhoods to rob and bring back the money so we could at least have cereal on the table.

I was learning to be evil. I didn't like seeing my brothers and sisters not having food. Not having small things like baloney for a sandwich or breakfast food really bothered me. Waking up and knowing your little brother and sister were hungry and there was only a box of Post Toasties on the table really disturbed me. And mom doing what she was doing, working really hard, sometimes eighteen hours on a dead end job, really made me into the person I became. The whole situation had an effect on me. My mom's life was horrible and became harder.

Things escalated, went from bad to worse and mom, I hate to say this, but mom had to become what she didn't want to become and she started selling herself just to feed us. That bothered me a lot. Her doing that made me more hateful towards people. I saw her struggle with her life and I didn't like seeing it.

It got to the point that when I saw guy after guy come and go, come and go, I started to rob them. When they left, I had the keys to their car. I said to them, "You are paying mom, now pay me." If they wanted their car back, they had to pay me. That is how I started stealing cars. I wasn't trying to be tough to them, I was just laying down my law: the strong survive. I took what I needed for my family. It didn't bother me that my brothers and I didn't have good shoes for school, but it did bother me when my sisters had to dress in dirty clothes or had no pretty barrettes for their hair as other kids did.

I was very protective of my sisters. When I was twelve my first arrest happened when I walked one of my sisters to the school bus and a white kid called her a "NB," I won't repeat the words. I was carrying a 25 automatic pistol and I turned around and shot the kid. I think he was fourteen or fifteen. I wasn't even phased. I was trying to get my sister on the bus so she could go to cheerleading practice and this kid called her those words. I shot him without thinking. I was arrested and put into Los Angeles Detention Center downtown, then transferred to MacLaren Hall with a bunch of other problem kids.

A cop we all called Big Red took me to the Hall. He was about six feet, seven inches tall, a big white cop in the gang task force, I mean this guy was big and when he was taking me to lock up, he told me I was too young to be doing the stuff I was doing. He said, "You don't seem like such a bad kid and I'm going to try to help you get a chance at life." He had taken a liking to me and was trying to help.

I took the chance he tried to give me, threw it away and said to myself, "OK, you're a sucker, I'll get over this one." His offer meant nothing to me. They kept me at MacLaren Hall for a year trying to rehabilitate me. But spending the time there only made me angrier.

After I was released from MacLaren, I got arrested again but this time I was sent to Camp David Gonzalez, a juvenile lockdown camp. It's in there I saw Big Red again and he said to me, "I hope you learn something this time."

But in that Camp as a young kid I learned something different than what he was trying to teach me: I learned to either fight or get beaten up. It was a tough place. I fought.

When I got home at thirteen, I was more violent than before. I had older friends who were in the South Central Crips and I wanted to be part of that lifestyle so I got it made known.

My initiation happened at a donut shop on one of the corners of Avalon in Los Angeles. Cops hung out there, they loved their donuts. I was thirteen years old and carrying a .32 caliber handgun. To show that I wanted to be a Crip, I walked up to a cop car parked at the donut shop and unloaded on it. There were people inside but I don't know to this day if anyone got hurt, I didn't stick around to find out. I never got arrested for that shooting.

All this jumping in today, the fighting with other gang members, that's not how it went down in my day. Our people wanted to know if you would cover their back in a gun battle, if you could perform and pull a trigger.

After I shot up the car, I got a lot of respect. But I didn't want to be just a part of the game, that wasn't my plan, I wanted to run the whole thing. Many of the guys were just into drinking, smoking and not really doing anything to help the community so I called some of the older homeboys out. I started initiating fights in order to see who was going to follow who, me or them. I wanted to be the leader and run the neighborhood so I fought for the title.

This time in my life at this young age, I became the most dangerous person I could be because I wanted people to follow me, respect me and do what I wanted them to do. I was the wolf. The older guys had to fight me, get with the program or one of us was going to get killed. Once we all had a meeting of the minds, I changed a lot of the priorities I wanted to make happen but most importantly I started running my neighborhood at sixteen years old.

CRIP is an acronym for Community Revolution In Progress. That's who we were and what we were about. I can honestly say that when I joined the Crips, they became my family, it was the first time I felt accepted. Because of that acceptance I wanted to become more and more respected in the gang. I did whatever it took to gain that respect. More and more of the kids who were older than me listened to me because I had no sympathy toward anything that wasn't connected to our community. What we needed to do we did, all in order to bring money into the neighborhood so that no one would be hungry. When I was around fourteen, if taking over a whole bus and robbing everybody on it was called for, or taking a restaurant down and robbing the people who were eating, we did it. Jewelry stores and their patrons were targets also, it didn't matter. I took back to the neighborhood whatever I got. It was a different culture then.

Today you have kids shooting and killing each other who don't know anything about the old culture or the real reason gangs were started. Much of the problem with gangs in the 1970's had to do with the media, the papers shined a light on us. With media pressure, the police started special units specifically to work against us.

I'm not trying to make what we were doing sound good because it wasn't. There were deaths, people got hurt, money was stolen but then drugs started coming into play, people started selling and a lot of money was being made. Along with the drugs came more trouble, more crime and more money to be fought over.

When I was fourteen because of my bad police record, I was placed into Washington High School, an all black, probationary school in Los Angeles. If a kid was convicted of a violent crime, he wasn't allowed to go to a regular school. Washington High was a Crip school. Across the city, Fremont High School was a Blood school. Crips and Bloods were rivals, deadly rivals. You had to go to a school which represented your gang affiliation to stay alive. If you went to a Blood school and you were a Crip, you'd be dead in a heartbeat. If you went to a Crip school and you were a Blood, same thing, you were dead. The authorities had to separate us, they had no choice if they wanted to avoid bloodshed.

This is why I can't be mad at the police because they did the best job they could to keep us away from each other and put everybody in safe schools. At least there wouldn't be a death every day. I wasn't thinking about it then, but when I look back on it now, the police were trying to minimize the deaths of young black kids. The kids were the ones pulling the triggers. The police were keeping us apart so that fewer mothers didn't have to go to a graveyard.

When I was at Washington High in the 12th grade, some of the guys I knew played football, some basketball. There were guys who could have been top tier college quarterbacks but because of their gang affiliations, they couldn't go to a university. I was one of the best three running backs in all of Los Angeles. Three schools recruited me but once they found out about my gang affiliations and gun use, they took all of their offers back. They didn't want me. Once again, here was something taken away from me and it just made me more angry. The angrier I became, the more violent I became.

By the time I was sixteen years old there wasn't anything I wouldn't do to hurt people, it didn't matter. I'll give you two examples, ones that I am not proud of.

First, there was a guy from the Westside who killed one of my home boys. We caught his sister. Killing him would would have been too good, too easy for him. We needed to bring hurt to his sister. So our gang raped the girl. Our thinking was that if we wanted to hurt someone, we wanted to do it where he would feel it the most. Usually that was his family. I was sixteen years old, running the Crips, encouraging gang rapes and I was a monster.

Second, I remember this old lady and the crime I committed against her. I took all her money just to hurt her grandson. She died about a week later because it was real cold and I don't think she had enough money to pay the electric bill. They found her dead in her house with no heat on. To this day, God is my witness, I feel remorse for taking money from that old lady. I feel sorry for that every day, I know God has forgiven me, but I still can't forgive myself for what I did to her. That crime, among all the others, will ride with me until the day I die.

I can't imagine today doing those things I did when I was young. I wish things were different, that I could erase the hurt I caused then. But I can't. I can only be forgiven by God.

I have to say something here. I thank God for my grandparents and to where God has brought me in my life. The only good things when I was young were my grandparents. My big mom and big dad kept telling me, "You gotta go to school, you gotta go to school." They were always pushing me. "Don't give up boy," they would say to me. "No matter what you do, don't give up." I could write well and began writing poetry at a young age. When I was at Washington High my grandparents pushed me to enter a poetry writing contest sponsored by the University of Southern California. I entered, sent them the poetry I had written and out of all the high schools from San Diego to Northern California, I won first place. I think that was the only good thing I ever did in those days.

My grandparents instilled Jesus in me at a young age, they planted the seed. They were always preaching Jesus. They were married seventy years. When I was around them I was in church or I was required to read the Bible. I knew about God and Jesus because of the influence they had on me. When I was with my grandparents it was either Sunday School or the belt so the easy decision was Sunday School. But all that teaching, all that time they put into me, went out the window when I went home to my mother, the alcoholism and drug addiction that was part of her life.

One day I will never forget, I was in grandma's garden helping her. She told me to dig deep, way down and pull the weeds out by their root. She loved growing collard and mustard greens but grass grew in her garden and it needed to be pulled out. I didn't want to pull grass so I just pulled it out a little bit, but she would say, "No boy, you gotta pull it out by the root because if you pull it out only a little bit, it's gonna grow back." I didn't think about what she was trying to teach me until some time later when I understood and it became clear to me. She planted a seed, the seed of Christ, deep within me that took root only when I got older. Had I only listened because the weeds in my life were growing.

Running with the Crips, leading them, when I was nineteen I got into a fight with a rival gang member and stabbed him seven times. I was arrested and sentenced to serve five years in New Folsom Prison, a California facility built especially to hold young guys like me. The sentence was lenient because had I stabbed someone not in a gang, I would have got a lot more time.

I did the whole five years in the Segregated Housing Program, or SHU, solitary confinement. The authorities didn't want me in general population because I was considered a bad influence, a threat to lead other kids to violence, even potentially doing harm to prison guards. So they kept me separated from others and in SHU.

In the SHU, there isn't a lot of television but sometimes a TV would have a program about church. I watched one Pastor, a Reverend talk about being lost and I thought that when I got out, I would visit him and he could set me on the right road to where I wouldn't be lost.

I got out when I was twenty-four years old and I really wanted to try and change my life. I found the Reverend's big old church in Los Angeles, and I was excited to think that maybe this church, this man, could help me get my life together.

I think back now and realize that this is where I really, really started to hate everything and everyone because when I went to see this man for guidance and help, mind you I'm fresh out of prison and I don't want to go back, I need help to change my life - and the man asked me how much money could I donate to his church! All I wanted was to talk to him, get some counseling but all he wanted was my money. I thought, man I'm from the streets, I don't make money unless I take it.

I left him and got mean in my thinking, the whole incident set me back. I ended up robbing the church two weeks later because of that question. I robbed everybody inside. I was that upset. I took everything I could get from the people. If someone could have taken the time to talk to me instead of asking me to fill out a bunch of forms and list how much money I made, things probably would have turned out differently. I went downhill fast after that; I went into a sinkhole. I was a loose cannon.

Around this time my cousin, whom I considered a brother, was killed by the police. He took up heroin after his mother, my Aunt Pearl, mom's sister, was hit and killed by a train. After her death, mom took in Aunt Pearl's kids, Ricky, Coco and Joanne. There were then eight kids in our home and mom had to feed all of us on a very limited income. That time was very hard on her.

Ricky and I took to the streets, we did everything together, it didn't matter what the crime was. We got involved in gang rapes, shootings, terrorizing families in their homes, like I said, it didn't matter. Ricky was a stone-cold killer, a first degree black belt, a hard man. He didn't need a gun, he could kill using his feet. When his mom was killed by the train, he became a very vile and evil person.

He started using heroin and over time, I saw what the drug did to him. Doctors told him that if he stopped using heroin he would die, his body was that dependent on the drug and his use had become that bad. Methadone wouldn't help him, he had to shoot heroin until the day he died which was the day he was shot by the police in a parking lot of a mall.

When Ricky was killed I really wanted to get my life together, change my environment, to at least try and be a better person. I was struggling with my reality. I moved from Los Angeles to Fort Worth, Texas. Texas offered former gang members help in getting Commercial Driver Licenses. I got my license and worked for Waste Management driving trash trucks for about one and a half years until I was twenty-five. The only job I've ever had but it didn't last long. If I could have stayed on course, I would be somewhere but instead I went somewhere.

All this time I was trying to stay away from the gang life. I thought everything was going to be better in Texas but the next thing I know I was around homeboys again.

The guys knew my name from California, a name carries itself as in, "Big D is down here." They knew of me and were saying my name so I started puffing my chest, wanting to be the big dog again, and right then I became the person I was trying to run away from. It seemed that everywhere I went, darkness followed me, it kept coming to me, there was no getting away from it. I didn't want to end up like my cousin Ricky but once again I found myself in a community of those who I once called family and there I went.

There was a shooting in Fort Worth where a twelve-year-old boy got shot. His dad was trying to buy drugs and he had his little boy in the car with him. That shooting caused a big commotion and trouble started between one side of Fort Worth, the Hoover Crips, and the other side, the Bloods. It became a bloodbath.

I became more and more involved, I lead the guys and got guns for everybody. I became more and more evil. I taught gang rapes because I wanted to inflict more harm and pain on the other side. I taught that if you shoot a guy, he can get over the bullet holes but if you do something that will impact his family it will last. The police wanted me badly for the gang rapes, more than any of the other crimes.

My little brother in the meantime had driven in from California with some drugs he was going to sell. He was more into selling dope than I was, he saw drug sales as a way to a better life. I really didn't care about selling dope. I'd rather just take the money, that was my thing.

After he arrived, he sold some weed laced with PCP, what we called 'Shermans' to a bunch of kids in Lufkin. The town is in East Texas. One of the kids, a local Judge's son, while smoking a Sherman drove into a telephone pole and unfortunately, killed himself.

About this time my brother and I had a run in with the Sheriff in Lufkin. Because I was mad at him, out of anger I shot and killed a bunch of cows on his ranch. He knew I shot them but he couldn't prove it.

So when I caught a rape case and was jailed in Fort Worth, the Lufkin Sheriff notified the arresting authorities, the Judge, the District Attorney and told them about me and what my brother and I had done in East Texas. I was never charged with killing the cows but it influenced the Judge and the Jury in Fort Worth, everything was piled on. They all knew where the Sherman came from, who killed the cows and who terrorized the town. The newspapers were full of the story: California boys terrorizing a peaceful city.

I was found guilty on multiple rape charges. That was when everything I ever did caught up with me, right then and there, all that I got away with over the years came down to that jury. In 1990, I was sentenced to serve ninety years in prison but the two cases, forty five years each, were to run concurrently, so I was to do forty five total and then and only then, would I be eligible for parole.

The State sent me to a prison called the Michael Unit, Tennessee Colony, Texas. There were three separate units there, all for the purpose of housing the States most violent offenders.

Comparing the SHU program in California to the Colony prison is like comparing the difference between day and night. When I was in California's SHU program, Charles Manson was locked up three cells down from me. Everything was pretty quiet. But in Texas there were a lot of people who wanted to be in the game, who wanted to prove they were tough, who didn't mind killing, stabbing or beating someone to death. I saw that all the time in Texas, not so much in California. Inside the Michael Unit, there were a lot of men who saw the violence, who weren't mentally able to deal with it so when they got out, they never came back. You could say that prison saved their lives.

Many people are familiar with the story of how in the late 1990's, this young white dude got out of prison, chained a black man named James Byrd to the back of his truck and dragged him to his death. The white dude who did it was raped repeatedly in prison. Do you think that had anything to do with him killing a black man? There are many stories like this of guys getting beaten and raped so many times that when they get out, they're filled with hatred and extreme violence.

In the Michael Unit because I was so violent, I was kept in a lockdown cell. I got out one hour a day for recreation. There were three white Correctional Officer Sergeants looking over guys on our tier who were constantly giving us a hard time. For instance, one of the guys on my block had seventeen days before his release but they kept going at him. My cell was on the top tier, level three of the building. One day these guys came up to my tier, my cell, with their batons in hand and they were looking to give me a beatdown, they were backing each other up. I knew what was going to happen when they slid the gate open.

Mind you, no Sergeant was authorized to open a gate on that tier, only a Lieutenant. I knew their intention so I rushed them and threw one of them off the tier. He fell to the floor below and broke his back. The two others then beat me senseless. That's why I'm blind in my right eye and my knees are so bad. They hogtied me and beat me almost to the point of death. My knees looked like pumpkin balls they were so swollen and my eye was hanging out of the socket. I had a big cut on my neck after it was over.

The next day a black Major came to work and he was told there was an incident in lockdown. He asked what happened and the guards tried to cover it up because again, no Sergeant was allowed to slide lockdown gates open. I was in the cell with my neck wide open, my eye still out and suffering the effects of the beating. After looking at me, the Major ordered that I be rushed to John Sealy Hospital in Houston where they gave me medical attention, took care of me and saved my life. It was a miracle that I survived.

I spent six months in the hospital. They wanted to take my eye out, it was so useless and painful. I had six surgeries trying to save it but they did no good. My eye had been popped and the doctors put it back in but I couldn't see out of it. I wanted to die, I didn't want to live anymore. I kept asking myself why, why, why all this pain. I couldn't understand my life because there was so much hurt. I had a lot of time to think.

After healing, they took me back to the Michael Unit. I was out of my cell for the one hour they allowed and two kids, Bloods, each close to nineteen years old, tried to make a name for themselves and kill me. They stabbed me in my hand when I put it up to stop one of the blows. I put both of them down within seconds and could have killed them but I didn't. They don't know how close they came to dying. The guards ran in, I got on my knees, threw the knife to them, they handcuffed me and took me to the hospital to take care of the knife wound. It sounds strange to say but I wanted those kids to really get after me but they didn't know what they were doing, they were kids.

When I was in the hospital I had a lot of time to think about all the people I ever hurt and everything I had done that was evil. I saw no light whatsoever in my life, only pure darkness. I wanted to end it all, I wanted to die.

After my release from the hospital I was taken back to my cell. The guards thought I was crazy and I was, so they put a sign on my door notifying white officers they were forbidden to approach my cell. That's what it came to, it would be a fight if a white man came close. When the sign went up I gave up on life, I didn't care about me, guards, nurses, chaplains, nobody. If you came into my space, there was going to be a fight. I didn't care who you were, I had no respect for anyone or anything.

There was a dark void in my life and my notice to everybody was stay away from me, let me die. I was through and I wanted to give up.

This is where my life changed.

I made a shank, a sharp homemade knife and I was going to kill myself. I couldn't take waking up every day with all the horrendous, horrible memories of what I had done constantly running through my mind. I had the knife under my pillow waiting for my time.

And that day, God can only explain it, there was a Bill Glass, Behind The Walls Prison Ministry going on in the yard with music loud enough that I could hear it. But the guys on lockdown weren't allowed to go, all the Crips, Bloods, people like that, couldn't be in general population.

I put my hand on the knife getting ready to use it … and there was a knock on my cell door. I looked up and there was this old white man staring through the bars right at me. I said to myself, "This fool has got to be crazy knocking on my door."

He said, "Son, I'm from Richardson, Texas. I wasn't going to come today but God told me there was someone who needed saving."

I remember those exact words. He then said, "I have walked this whole prison but it was you when I walked up to your cell door, it was you."

I took my hand off of the knife.

I know people won't believe this, what I am about to say, they think I made this up, but the face that I was looking at was not a human face, it was the face of an angel.

I cannot explain how I let this white man talk to me through that cell door about Christ but that is what happened. His name was Mr. Henry Sorelle. And this was the turning point in my life. He said, "Listen, they told us not to give anybody our phone number or our address. But I need you to have my address. I need you to write me, to communicate with me. I want to help you."

That day in 1995 at 3:27 pm, he reached through the bars, took me by the hands on bended knees and he prayed with me through the bars, through the cell door.

I gave my life to Christ there and then with Mr. Henry Sorelle and me praying on our knees to God. When I got up, for the first time in my life I saw light, I saw light! That was a miracle in itself. A God thing. When God is involved it doesn't take long for things to work.

The next morning I sent word out to all the homeboys that I was through, done. I wasn't going to give orders for anything. I told them that if I had taken anything from them, I would give it back. Word came back to me that they thought I was crazy.

About ten days after I gave my life to Christ, a Corrections Officer, Major Wheat, came to me and asked if I wanted to go to general population. I looked at him and thought he was playing with me. Things like that don't normally happen but they released me from the lockdown cell and put me into the yard.

I wasn't there long when they decided to ship me off the Michael Unit and move me to general population in the Estelle Unit in Huntsville. This is where things got interesting. I was stunned for a while. I was looking at things from a new perspective because of my acceptance of Christ and I didn't like the way things were going down in Estelle. There were so many fights, K2 smoking and drugs everywhere in that place. I asked myself what I could do to change things so I wrote my mentor Mr. Sorelle and asked him what I should do.

He sent me a letter and told me that I had to bring people together in the right way. With that advice, I went to the Warden and told him, "Look, I know I have a bad reputation but I would like to try something." He asked me, "What," and I said, "Let me run the intramural games in the Unit and I promise I will make it work."

He said, "We tried that, there were too many fights, we've tried all kinds of programs but they never go right." I wasn't trying to brag but I told him, "It wasn't me doing it," I was thinking of God, "Let me see if I can't make it work."

I got the gang leaders together and told them that as long as there was chaos, they were going to have police or guards in their lives constantly and they knew that to be true. You have to meet people where they are. So they tried what I was selling and as I began to teach and lead them, I began to bring Christ into their lives.

I give God all the Glory but with work and effort the program we put into place became successful, so successful that the model is still in place today. I pulled all the leaders on the Unit together and told them we were going to start playing games and in order to do that, guys had to stop catching cases, stop with the Disciplinary Reports, they couldn't fight or do the drugs. I had a lot of pushback but then when everybody started having fun and the Warden was bringing hamburgers and pizzas to the games, more and more people wanted to get involved.

We had the west side of the building versus the east side or the south side. We had basketball and soccer games. I put together relay races, different volleyball games, Badminton tournaments but there always one rule: there had to be one white, one black, one hispanic, one asian, every nationality had to be represented on a team. A team of one race wasn't allowed. This bonded guys together and as we started playing these games, the fights became less, the anger issues went down.

I was writing my mentor Mr. Sorelle, telling him about the progress we were making and he suggested that I start writing my words and thoughts down so they could be copied, handed out and read by men who couldn't hear me in person, in other words, men in other prisons.

I guess soon after, something I had written got to a woman named Nancy Peters. She worked in Utah and ran the Allstate Insurance Company for the entire State. She told me she heard about what I was doing and asked me how she could help. I realized that all I had to do was write a paper, send it to Mr. Sorelle, he would send it to Ms. Peters, she would make thousands of copies for free and send them out to other prisons. I didn't have money to make copies and get them distributed. The cost of the stamps, envelopes and paper had to be thousands and thousands of dollars. She sent me a typewriter and I used that to type my messages. I was able to reach people in other prisons with the messages. How did all this come to me? It was God, I had nothing, but God had everything.

One day a letter arrived from a Mr. and Mrs. Rohrer, ex-college professors, teachers living in Pennsylvania, offering to help edit the papers I was writing. To this day they continue to help me. Mrs Rohrer told me, "Just send your papers to us and we will edit them and help you." I began to write and I asked God, "God, how do I do this, I don't know what I'm doing," but God knew.

Some of the gang members in the Unit saw what I was doing and asked me what this "Jesus thing" was about. There you go, God's in charge. So I met people on their battleground and that was where swords were thrown down but one sword was picked up. They began throwing down the swords of evil and picking up the sword of truth, the Bible. I started to get Bibles sent to me so I could hand them out.

Some of the guys couldn't read so we started a reading program and it progressed to where guys were getting their GED through an educational program.

There were men inside sentenced to hundreds of years, lifers who were never getting out and they were coming to me saying, "Hey man, I can read now, I can write now, thank you!" To me that was worth more than a million dollars because I told them that if they could read, then they could read the Bible and start getting their life together. I told them to write their kids, write their families and tell them what God had accomplished in their lives. I was no longer a person out to hurt but a person out to heal. I wanted to help people be better human beings.

Today, I ask people all the time, "Can you tell me the one time that Jesus turned away somebody who wanted to be with Him?"

It's in the Gospel of Mark. Jesus healed a man who was living in tombs. His community knew him and kicked him out, they tried to chain him down but nothing could hold him. Then he met Jesus, and his life changed so much that he wanted to follow Jesus, "Let me go where you go," he asked, but Jesus said, "No, you go back and tell others what great things the Lord has done for you."

I live by that principle today because the favor of God is upon me. I follow Jesus and He has taught me to go back to the very people I hurt. I don't want people to misread this, I go back because I should be in a grave right now but by the grace of God, His Son saved me, He saved my life. I should be dead and therefore I cannot help but tell others what great things God has done for me and how grateful I am for having had Mr. Sorelle in my life.

When things were going along well, a bad day came when the Warden called me and the Major into his office. They knew Mr. Sorelle and the difference he had made not only in my life but the impact he had on the entire prison environment. The Warden told me Mr. Sorelle had passed away. We were all very sad, I didn't know how my life was going to go on. I was allowed to call his wife Francis from the office and there were a lot of tears. I didn't know what I was going to do.

During the time Mr. Sorelle and I had been writing each other, I had written seven little pamphlets, little books that were published by a Christian Organization and distributed to other prisons. After Mr. Sorelle passed, people who never met me face to face Mr. and Mrs. Rohrer, and Ms. Peters, helped me even more. It was God's timing. They helped me get the messages out that I was writing. I didn't have any money but God did, He provided those people to help me. That was all Him.

Then one day out of nowhere, another miracle happened. I got a letter from a Pastor Terry Northway. He told me that God had put it on his heart that he had to help me, that I should continue to write messages of how God saved me and he would get the messages sent to other prisons. He never met me but trusted in God. Pastor Terry to this day has a prison ministry in Santa Fe, New Mexico, and he wanted to use what I was writing to help reach prisoners there. He made sure I had stamps and funds to do all that I wanted or needed. My typewriter broke and he bought me another one. He had people on his team to help me and we work together to this day.

Around the year 2010, when he was still alive and five years after he led me to Christ, Mr. Sorelle had talked about how after I got out, he would buy a halfway house and we would run it together. He wanted to help people get their lives together after release. This was ten years before I was released and he was telling me how I would get out and make this idea work, as God is my witness. He planted a seed. But then he passed away and as I said, at his death my life had no direction.

In the year 2020 I had been in prison since 1990, thirty years. I wasn't eligible for parole until 2035 and wasn't even thinking about parole, the thought never crossed my mind. I knew nothing about getting paroled. All I wanted to do was change the lives of people in prisons. God had changed my life and I wanted to make that happen for others but to be honest, I still believed I was going to die in prison. My focus was writing published messages to make lives better, one at a time, because that is what my mentor Mr. Sorelle taught me.

I went before the Parole Board in 2020 and again, another God miracle. One Board Member was the deciding vote and I got a release date of July 21, 2020. I had spent 30 years in prison. I walked out of a past life and into a new one.

I was assigned to a halfway house where the living conditions were horrible: drugs, animosity, dirt, filth and the people running it were in it only for the money. There were two houses together and the community they were in was run by a home-owners association. The houses were in a really nice area but the people living in the community were protesting the conditions. I had just moved in and one day was talking to a real estate agent who was visiting the property and she told me the owner was catching a lot of flak and was going to sell both of them.

I called Pastor Terry and told him the situation. Mind you, he had never met me personally, he trusted in God for me to do the right thing if he got involved. Pastor Terry told me. "You talk to the people and tell them we are going to buy the houses," just like that and then he says, "You can run them," again, just like that! My mentor's prophecy came to pass.

Pastor Terry made a deal with the owner and paid $380,000 cash for both houses. He then sent me more cash and said, "Clean 'em up," and with some work, we turned both of them into the best half-way houses within a 500-mile radius in the State of Texas. All by the grace of God.

After the purchase was made, I was cutting grass in the yard and this girl walked by, looked at me and asked me for my phone number. She asked me, "What black man nowadays cuts the yard?" I laughed because I was out exercising and doing therapy on my legs but she gave me her sister's phone number and told me, "Look, my sister hasn't dated anyone for thirteen years. We are trying to find her someone good and you look like a good person." I never heard that before, but I was given her name, Sherlyn, and her number. Her sister told me she was a District Missionary of her Church, the Mims Church of Christ here in Austin.

I called her but the first time but she didn't answer. I called her a second time and still no answer. I was persistent and I called a third time and she answered. During our conversation she told me that she had never been married and I told her that I hadn't either. She said in the past, she had told God that she was tired of being single.

She came to see me after we talked on the phone. She told me she wanted someone in her life, but when she had told God, He told her she had to wait because, "he hadn't gotten out yet."

That's what she told me, that God said to her that her man hadn't gotten out yet! She said to me, "I want this, I'm telling you right now, let me look at you when I tell you this but I need to tell you something first. I love the Lord Jesus Christ. He is first in my life. If you can't accept this, then we can't be together, we can't even start talking."

I knew this was good, that she was the kind of woman I wanted. We met on May 18th, 2021, and got married September 29, 2022. We committed to having no physical relations before we got married. We wanted to follow God's plan and be blessed together as husband and wife. It was difficult at first for me because I had been gone thirty years and Satan was there trying me.

Today she is my best friend first and my best wife second. She is a wonderful woman who begins every day with scripture reading between four and six in the morning. At first I didn't understand fully, she sometimes would have questions about what she was reading and ask me for help to understand. I told her I wasn't a Bible teacher but I could explain it from a street sense, so I did. What I brought to her was a new understanding, one that she was able to take to the streets of Austin as part of her missionary work.

People all over Austin love this lady because she is the sweetest lady around. It was unbelievable to me that God would put someone like her into my life. Who am I that God would do that?

The business we do today in the halfway houses is to help guys who are newly released find a job, open a bank account and teach them how to start looking for their own apartment. We educate them to be the men God created them to be. My passion today, besides my wife, is helping guys inside and out find Jesus. I meet with families of men regularly, mothers of sons locked up who are trying to get their family members out of prison and into our program. We have a waiting list of more than three hundred. Between the two houses, there are a limited number of beds so we work with what we have. There is a great need for a women's house also.

I went to a women's shelter in Austin with one of the ladies of my church and the experience just broke my heart. I looked at the battered and bruised women who have given up on life and who need hope restored. I shared some of my story with them and I always share hope. These women have gone through a lot of turmoil trying to keep their families together, trying to get on their feet, get jobs and I'm honored to be able to have them trust me enough to let me help them. If they knew all the story of my former life, who I was and what I was, they would probably have been scared. But there is always hope to share and love to spread. I am the new Alonzo Dixon and I am doing what God and His Son Jesus Christ has intended for my life.

Alonzo and his beautiful wife, Sherlyn, live in Austin, Texas, and continue everyday to live out God's plan for their marriage and future which is embodied in Gospel truth, Romans 8: 37-39.

"Yet, in all these things we are more than conquerors through Him who loved us. For I am convinced that neither death nor life, neither angels nor principalities, neither the present nor the future, nor any powers, neither height nor depth, nor anything else in all creation, will be able to separate us from the love of God that is in Christ Jesus our Lord."

Please find below a letter written to prisoners when Alonzo was still in a Texas high security prison. The letter shows the depth of his love and the height of his belief in Christ.

FAILURE NEVER MEANS DEFEAT

Greetings to all brothers and sisters behind prison walls. It is by the grace of God and our Lord Jesus Christ that I share these words with all of you. Words of encouragement and comfort; words of inspiration and reassurance to bring you hope and to help build your faith as you stand firm in your commitment to Christ. Satan will have you believe that there is no hope and that all is lost. But keep your eyes on the prize, which is Jesus Christ, our Lord and Savior, and you will realize that through faith, **failure never means defeat.**

In this material world in which we live we often mistake confidence for faith. We become confident in our own ability, forgetting that our strongest moments can sometimes be deceptive. This is not faith, but a false sense of confidence. When trials and disasters arise that are beyond our own power to control we begin to sink in misery and despair. We begin to cry out to the Lord for help. It is in these weak moments that we can be strong in Him. It is through our faith that He showers us with His grace, and it is because of our faith in Jesus Christ that we realize that in Him **failure never means defeat.**

Please open your Bibles to Luke 22:31-32. Then read verses 54-62. Peter was the disciple that may have been the strongest of them all. He stood out among them in many ways. Peter was the first to look Jesus in the eyes and say, **"You are the Christ, the Son of the Living God."** (Luke 9:20).

It was Peter who stood among them and put Jesus to the test saying, **"Lord, if it is you, tell me to come to you on the water."**(Matthew 14:28).

It was Peter who left home, wife and business to follow Jesus (Mark 1:16-17; Luke 18:28-29).

Because of Peter's status with the other disciples he became filled with confidence as we see when he looks at Jesus and says, **"Lord, I am ready to go with you to prison and to death."** (Luke 22:33).

It is with confidence that Peter makes these statements. It is with self-assurance that he stands on his own. However, when disaster comes into Peter's life things change. Here was Jesus, the man Peter walked with, talked with, broke bread with, and to whom Peter had committed his life, turning around and denying him three times in one night (Luke 22:57-60).

To put it plainly, Peter failed in his faith. But in his failure there was no defeat. Peter cried out for forgiveness in John 21 and Jesus forgives him and reinstates him as a trusted disciple. Later it was Peter who takes the lead among the disciples and then it was he who preaches the first sermon after the Holy Spirit fell at Pentecost and over 3,000 were saved. It was Peter that God called to lead the first Gentiles to faith in Christ (Acts 10).

And it was Peter who was later killed for his faith in Jesus Christ. As we understand the life of Peter, he becomes an example that **failure never means defeat.**

Brothers and sisters, every day we are faced with temptations and stumbling blocks. Every moment of every hour of every day of the week of every month of every year Satan, our enemy, prowls around like a roaring lion seeking those he may devour. We have all failed in life. Some of us are living our lives behind prison walls. But do not lose hope. Never give up. Because we have fallen does not mean we are defeated. Let us all lay our past at the cross of Jesus Christ. We cannot allow others to bring us down. We cannot let the negative talk of others outweigh the positive truth in knowing Jesus Christ. Let us all hold on the faith. We have a promise from Jesus Himself where he says, **I will never leave you or forsake you.** (Hebrews 13:5).

You must remember that we can do all things through Christ who strengthens us. (Phil.4: 13).

In His Name we are more than conquerors.

Brothers and sisters, many of us have failed in life. We have hurt our families and our children. We have hurt others and hurt our communities. In spite of our many failures, now is the time to give up trying to do things our way. It is time to step up and stand up. Right now is the time to confess your sins (Romans 10:9-10).

It is with the blood of Jesus that we fight against the strong arm of Satan. It is with His blood that we stand firm when our flesh is weak. It is with unwavering faith that we look to the hills from whence comes our help. When the day seems dark and our way is obscured, it is through faith that we hold on. No matter how far we have fallen, we can step out boldly on the troubled waters because as long as we have faith in Jesus Christ our **failure will never mean defeat.**

Written by: Alonzo Dixon 706677
Estelle High Security Unit
Huntsville, TX 77340

8

"A Scream and Then…"

"We are all prisoners of our own making, confined by the choices we've made." **Sharyn McCrumb**, The Ballad of Frankie Silver (Ballad #5)

Aquil Phillip had a desire one night to kill someone. He made the decision, planned the outcome and the events turned out that someone died - but that death was not the one he had planned.

AQUIL PHILLIP
Death Or Prison podcast, Numbers 100 and 101
13 years inside

I was born in Brooklyn, New York, in 1987. My mom and dad were from Trinidad. My mom wanted to leave Brooklyn because the neighborhood we lived in was crime infested, really bad and besides, she didn't like the cold winters. Mom and dad were never married so when mom split from my dad she moved to Florida with me and my older brother Jamal. I was five years old.

We landed in Fort Pierce, lived there for one and a half years then moved to Port St. Lucie, a kind of secluded area totally different than what I was used to. My father wasn't around and I missed him.

My brother and I were fighting a lot, arguing as brothers do but I looked up to him because he was seven years older than me and again, my father wasn't around.

I loved watching Bruce Lee movies, I loved the cultures of the Japanese and Chinese so I decided to study martial arts, that became my thing. I started eating with chopsticks and my brother was all over me for that, he kept saying, "Man you're not Chinese," and I would tell him to leave me alone, I was trying to be like Bruce.

One night when I was six, something happened to my family that had great impact on me for years to come. My mother got a phone call and when she hung up she came into our bedroom and was crying. I was in the top bunk bed, my brother on the bottom and mom was crying profusely so I started to cry. I didn't even know what was wrong but she told me to get down and she then told both of us that dad had been shot and killed in Brooklyn. We broke down together, the three of us, sobbing, crying and holding each other.

I remember that moment because something inside of me broke and when it broke, I really hurt. I felt anger and pain at the same time. As a result of hearing my dad had died, when I went back to school, anytime anyone would say anything about my parents, my father especially, immediately I would fight. If I came home and told my mom about the fight she would be mad at first but then she would calm down and say to me something like, "You're doing good at school, you have to stop fighting, you're too smart to be doing stuff like that."

But I didn't stop. I lashed out at everybody, my mom and all the people around me. When I was in school and doing the work, I was getting A's and B's but then I would get into a fight and get suspended. I was talking back to teachers, running away from them when they would call me. I was on a downward spiral because I didn't have guidance or anyone to put me on the right path. I stopped listening to my mom, she had very little influence on me. My older brother was in the same rut, he wasn't fighting as much as I was but he started leaning towards doing drugs.

I had an aunt who lived in Rochester, New York, and I would go visit her sometimes in the summer or in the winter for Christmas. I remember the first time I ever paid attention to hearing anything about God or Jesus was in her house, she was always talking about them. She had kids and the only thing they were ever allowed to watch were programs that had a God or Jesus theme. I thought that it was weird that we couldn't watch regular television. Over the course of time I heard the Gospel and I thought to myself that I didn't disbelieve the teaching, it sounded alright but I pushed it away from me.

My godmother lived in Staten Island, New York, and she was always talking about God too. So when I would visit her or talk to her on the phone she would encourage me to learn about God but I think I was too young to understand the concept that God loved me. I found later in life that God sends messengers to us, words that if we don't take heed to we will later regret the results of not listening.

The fighting continued in school while at the same time my mother was struggling financially. Because of money trouble, she decided to move us from Port St. Lucie further south to Broward Count. I was about seven or eight years old when we arrived in an area that was more hood than urban. There were gangs, drugs and prostitution, all of which made me more curious about what I saw but scared me too. I was scared of my mom first off because I didn't want the belt but my curiosity peaked on what was going on in the world.

In the new school, I started to like football. I could run fast and had good hands so I got on the team and played wide receiver and running back. I got better and better at football and saw it as something I could do with my life. I discovered I was good at basketball too and started playing heavily. My brother in the meantime, was dating a stripper who could get bottles of liquor and when she came to visit, she often brought them along.

Now I was exposed to liquor and I began drinking occasionally. My brother convinced me that I could sell the bottles his girlfriend was bringing us, so in high school I became the liquor man and started selling to the kids. I carried them in my book bag, went to certain spots on the grounds and sold them to kids. I tried selling dope one time but that didn't work out.

I started to notice girls for the first time, my focus had changed and I started messing around. I was playing basketball for money, shooting dice and getting sucked into the world. A few years prior, my mother got saved. She stopped drinking, started praying regularly, reading her Bible and talking to me about God. It was the same as listening to my aunt from Rochester.

I noticed her change, the way she would go to work, go to church, go to work, and I thought how boring, I didn't want a life like that, it wasn't for me. She talked about God but what she said deterred me rather than convinced me, I knew it was real for her but I didn't want it for me. The Bible says the flesh is never satisfied and I was an example of that truth. I got into gambling heavily and kept going deeper into the world, I wanted more and more of what the ways of the flesh offered. I started listening to music about murder, drugs, getting money and I felt like I was lacking in my life because I didn't have any money. I was seventeen years old. Mom used to make me think $20 was a lot of money but I knew it wasn't. I knew I had to get some money so I took a job at Target but I quit after a week. Then I worked at Papa John's for about three months, was still selling the liquor but the whole plan wasn't working, I wasn't making enough money. I decided I could make more if I took to the streets. With some friends I started stealing from different places. The guys I was with then got some guns so we progressed to the point where we started talking about doing robberies.

God was still trying to get my attention through my mom. We were driving home from church one day, she had forced me to go because it was African Day and we were dressed up in African clothes. We were turning left in a lane with the green arrow and a car crashed hard into us. We both were jerked around, she got out to inspect the damage, went to the back of the car and was saying, "Oh, thank you Lord, thank you Lord!" I couldn't understand why she was going crazy so I got out and went to the back. My mom had a 626 Mazda, a car that's not known to be solid and the other car was an SUV. Mom's car only had scratches but the SUV looked totaled, it looked like it had run into a crash dummy wall.

Mom was telling me, "Do you see how God is protecting us? This is why I am always telling you about God, He sent His angels to protect us." When I looked at the cars and compared the damage, I said to myself, "God is definitely real. It's true what mom has been saying." The whole experience captivated me.

The next day nothing had changed in my thinking, I was still the same person I was before the accident. Mom's statements didn't stick, I wanted to continue to do what I was doing with my friends, robbing and stealing. One Friday night we decided to rob some dudes who had just got off of work and were hanging out together. We drove and got the shotgun.

Around 2006 when this was about to go down, the dress code on the street was super long shirts people called "Tall Tees." I put the shotgun under the Tall Tee, we were creeping up on the men we were going to rob and I then saw a lady open a door near them. A little girl came outside and stood beside the lady. I still had a conscience and a heart I guess, because of what mom had been putting into me but there was a battle always going on in me. As soon as I saw the little girl I told my friends, "No, no, no, we can't, not now." My conscience got to me so we left.

On a different night we tried to rob another guy but he got away. He ran into a parking lot and was lucky because we had baseball bats and we were going to beat him, totally crush him. I was an angry young man wanting to do damage.

This next story will tell you the low level of my thinking. I was in the eleventh grade and I owned a popular DVD. I gave the DVD to a friend who then gave it to my best friend. My best friend lied to me and told me he never got it back so I went to the guy I originally gave it to and pressed him but he told me the truth, that he had given it back. I didn't believe him and I was going to stab him.

My other friend who had lied to me then tried to discourage me from that route, he told me, "No man just go fight him like you normally do,"

Long story to short, that night I got on my bike and was planning on stabbing him. I had brass knuckles also on me. I rode my bike to where the guy worked and I planned to wait in some bushes for him to get off, then I was going to jump him but I got there late by about five or ten minutes. Thank God the guy had already left. So I rode my bike to where my best friend was working. I told him what had gone down and he asked me if I was crazy, wanting to stab a guy over a DVD.

The next morning my best friend called me and said, "Man, I'm sorry man, I lost your DVD, I just didn't want to tell you, but man I'm going to give you money for it, don't worry."

In hindsight, at seventeen years of age I would have stabbed an innocent guy over nothing he had done. He had told me the truth, he had given it to my best friend but my mindset was tormented. Thank God, He intervened.

My mindset after that actually got worse, I kept getting angrier, more distraught and about this time my mom and I had a falling out over something my brother did but I didn't want to tell her anything. She blamed me for what he did and she hit me in the head with a broomstick. I got mad, went out the door and slammed it hard. To my mind, I was done living with her, I was seventeen, old enough I figured, to be on my own. My brother told me to chill, walk around the block and calm down but it didn't work. I thought I knew everything about the world, about everything that was going on. But guess what, one week later I was back with her on a Friday night.

That night she told me I had to go to church with her, a church called Redeeming Word. I got into the car really angry, partly because I had to return to living with her. I started to beat the seats with my hands, I was possessed and I cried. When I cried my mom began to pray because she had never seen that much emotion from me before. As she prayed, my whole body locked up, I couldn't beat the seats anymore and I really couldn't move. My body felt like it was on fire and I couldn't cry or move, my body was being kept still. We got to the church, she parked the car and told me to follow her inside.

We got out of the car and I let her walk in front of me. I couldn't go inside so I ran from her to a market I knew around the block. I stayed at the market the whole time I figured she was at church, then I returned to the car. She probably didn't know I didn't attend because she was so mad. She was walking to the car when I approached her and that is when I knew right then that something had hold of me, something more powerful than me had me bound, an enemy had me. From then on I couldn't go into a church or even be around a church setting.

That is when my mind switched from wanting to do robberies to wanting to do a murder. I wanted to kill. I was listening to some really evil music and the influence of the lyrics had me spiritually, demonically bound.

Three of my friends and I were going to do a robbery one night soon after that time I had with mom at the church. We had a plan in our heads but the Bible says, "There is a way that appears right unto a man but the end thereof is death." I've learned that anytime evil is planned, there will always be a backfire.

Four of us were riding around looking for someone to rob and we saw a guy in his car talking on his phone. Before we hopped out we drove around looking for the right time and I told my friends, "If anybody acts crazy, I'm going to kill him."

I spoke that thought from my mouth not knowing the power of my words. I said just that.

We returned to where he was parked and we backed our car in beside his car. The parking lot had parking barriers, ledges, but there were no other cars around. I got out with the shotgun in my hands. I went to the guy's car, pointed the shotgun at him and said, "Give it up!" The guy started to panic. My friends were searching his pockets, he began to really panic and completely lost it. I was going to kill him, I had that thought in my mind and I got closer with the shotgun pointed at him.

Suddenly he let out a scream that to this day I have never heard anybody scream like that, it was a Reaper scream, the spirit of death yelling and when he screamed, he tried to jump and grab the barrel of the shotgun. I went backwards over one of the parking barriers and the gun went off. The guy fell down.

Two of the guys with me began to run, I grabbed the gun and I turned to run also. As I turned, I looked back at the guy who I had intended to rob and kill but he's getting up. I wondered, "How is he getting up?"

I ran to the car, threw the shotgun in but my two friends start yelling, "You shot C, you shot C." After the shot, C had dropped on the pavement and we all went out to get him. We picked him up but he had a big hole in his chest where the blast hit him. We got him into the backseat of the car and I held him in my arms saying to him all the time, "Hold on, hold on, hold on." One of the other guys was driving like crazy and he was crying.

As I held C and telling him to hold on, he breathed his last breath. I heard it go out. Immediately I had flashbacks of every time something that had happened to me such as the car crash with mom or someone in the past had talked to me about God, it all flashed before my eyes, my whole life flashed when he died as I held him in the backseat of that car.

We made it to the hospital and I was in shock, I couldn't think clearly. C was dead on arrival, he was gone. They brought a stretcher to the car, took him inside and tried to revive him but what they did didn't work. Police were at the hospital, put the three of us together and asked us a bunch of questions about what had happened.

We made up a story of how some dudes tried to rob us but C tried to resist and got shot in the process. They let us go so I went to my friend's house where I had been living. Remember I had stopped talking with my mom and had moved out of her house about three months before. During those months I had been living on the streets and in my friend's house, surviving by committing robberies, that's how I was getting money.

I was in shock for the whole night, constantly asking myself what had happened, what had gone wrong. Four of us were doing a robbery like we had done before and I ended up taking a life, not the one I wanted to take, the life of one of my friends. People in the house tried to talk to me but I couldn't respond because I was thinking of what had happened, what had gone wrong and trying to process everything but I was still in shock and unable to think or talk.

I don't know how I fell asleep but the next day I woke up to the guy I was staying with and his mom crying, standing beside him. I looked outside, I saw the Detective who had talked to us from last night coming to the front door and knocking. As he was knocking I was panicking, wondering what he was doing at the house, we had given our statements at the hospital and I was telling myself to hold on, keep it together.

My friend and his mother went to the door and I was looking for a way to escape but there was no escape, no way out. We all ended up going down to the station where we were put in a cold room with a lot of cameras. A policeman came and grabbed my friend for an interview. They were gone for about two hours and as time went on, I figured he was telling them everything that had happened. They then came and got me, put me in a room and I told them what I told them at the hospital, that somebody tried to rob us and C tried to fight back, to buck the robbery but the guys killed him.

The police told me they knew that wasn't how it all went down, they knew about our intended victim, a Hispanic male, that what I told them wasn't the real story, it was all a lie. They knew I had thrown the shotgun in a lake after the incident and they had divers right then searching for it.

After they told me everything that had happened because they knew the truth, I confessed, I told them I did it. They brought papers for me to sign and put me in handcuffs. They called my mother and about twenty minutes later she came through the door. I remember her face, I will never forget, she was crying. Everything inside of me shook, it all hit me, what

I had done, I started to cry, and she came to me asking, "What happened, what happened?"

I told her everything, that I had done it, and after I was through confessing to her, she started praying. While I was growing up she had prayed over me many times, she had anointed me with oil, she had laid her hands on me but while I was in handcuffs, she and I began praying together. She literally prayed me into the Kingdom at that moment. While I was in handcuffs, I can't stress that enough.

I was arrested physically but after that prayer, I felt as though the Holy Spirit had arrested me at the same time. I gave my heart, my soul, my life to Jesus Christ while I was in handcuffs. I told God, "I surrender. I've been running from you but from now, on I give my life to Christ." That moment was the start of something beautiful that came out of a terrible tragedy.

When I gave my heart to Jesus, I felt lifted, a sense of peace came to me, God got me. I knew it was a bad situation I had gotten into, I had killed someone and I was in handcuffs for committing a major crime. I didn't know what was going to happen to me from then on but my mother started to encourage me, telling me that God could work His way even in this bad situation. She told me to start reading the Word, the Bible, and really surrender to Him. I told her, "Yes, yes," because her words were like a belt to me, a worse belt than what the handcuffs were doing to me. I had never been arrested or in handcuffs before and this whole thing hit me like a ton of bricks.

After the paperwork and prayers, the police took me to the main jail where I was booked. They read the charges to me: Unpremeditated murder in the first degree and attempted armed robbery with a deadly weapon. Punishable by life in prison.

I got to make a phone call to my mom after I was booked and I told her the charges. She knew she had to be strong so she encouraged me. "Listen," she said, "Trust God, I hear your charges but I need you to trust

God." I told her I would. She told me to read the Bible and to not stop praying.

They did a strip search on me, gave me a change of clothes and took me to the third floor of the jail. I slept for three hours when they woke me and took me to the sixth floor. They had given me brown prison clothes and were about to put me in with the guys in the first pod who also had on brown clothes so I figured I was where I was supposed to be. But the Officer looked at my entry card and told me I was in the wrong pod, that I needed to go to number three pod.

I walked into number three, they all had on zebra stripes and they all looked like gorillas. My thought was, "Lord, I know what I've seen on TV and I'm not letting anybody take anything from me. I will fight and thank you God, I know how to fight." I was fearful, I was thinking of all that I had heard and seen in movies. I said to myself, "Nah, I'm not going to let that happen, I'm not letting them take anything from me, they'll have to kill me."

I was taken to a cell on the top floor of the pod, the second tier, room two. I walked into the cell, put my stuff down and I looked at my roommate thinking, "Okay, I have to fight," and he said to me, "Man, that's crazy," and I asked him, "What's crazy?" And I put my foot back because I don't know what was coming. He says, "I saw what happened with you, y'all made the news."

He hopped down off of his bunk and went into his bin. He pulled out a newspaper and gave it to me. There was my story written in headlines, everything that had happened. The year was 2006. I got comfortable with him, I realized he wasn't a threat. We talked and I learned he had a cousin who had been ministering to him so he had been finding his way to a relationship with God. No coincidence that I was in his cell, right? I found that God led me to a right situation and I started reading the Bible as my mother told me, not understanding it but reading it.

On a phone call I told my mother that I wasn't getting anything the Bible was saying, a lot of 'Thees' and 'Thous', I was lost. She told me that before I read, I needed to pray for wisdom, knowledge and understanding. So I did, I followed her instruction and the next time I read, it made sense to me. I got a couple different versions and as I read more and more, something inside of me became transformed, my mindset started to change. One of the small changes was that I wanted to stop cussing.

My roommate was transferred and a new one arrived. He was a Christian, I thanked God for blessing me and I told my new roommate that I was trying to get closer to God. He told me he was too. We both felt God had put us together for a purpose. Both of us wanted to stop cussing so we took the initiative and were intentional. We planned between us that if we cussed, we had to do twenty squats. In the beginning we were doing hundreds of squats, daily, we developed strong legs so we switched to pushups. The Bible told us that we needed to renew our minds, it was a process and the renewing didn't come immediately, we had to work at it. We also prayed about the renewing and eventually our vocabulary started to get cleaner because of the practical steps we took to make it happen.

I struggled with the renewing of my mind in one area especially: I always carried a chip on my shoulder for the man who killed my father, I had un-forgiveness in my heart. Before I ever was locked up I had looked the guy up on the internet and found him. He was living in California but got locked up for a crime he had done. I found his release date.

I made a plan with my fourteen year old brother to kill the guy the day he got out. I was seventeen. My brother was all for the plan. We didn't know that vengeance was the Lord's. We never put the plan into action but I carried this hardness of heart with me.

After I got arrested and had asked Jesus into my life, I asked the Lord to forgive me for all the crimes, all the sin I ever committed, the Lord said to me, "You want me to forgive you but if you don't forgive men of what they did to you, how can I forgive you of all you did to me?" I was really struck by God's words. In my mind I was trying to change but God confronted me to forgive the guy who killed my father.

My mind said, "No." Truthfully I wanted to slaughter the guy. But in my heart, in my spirit, God was convicting me and bringing me to a position where I had to humble myself and surrender. It took three days of me fighting with God on this issue of forgiveness. At the end of the third day, I told God that I surrendered, that I let the guy go and everyone else who ever did me wrong I forgave.

When I forgave everyone I felt a release, I felt light, my body felt light, my mind felt light. I didn't know I was going through a process that would lead to my freedom. God was freeing my mind and my heart, He was freeing me from enslavement. When all of this was happening I was being raised to another level of seeking God because the un-forgiveness that I let go of was no longer in my way, blocking me.

One of the guys I had done the crime with and a codefendant, was transferred from the juvenile floor to the adult floor, the one I was on. I had been in County Jail for almost a year, had turned eighteen and was going to be charged as an adult. The Prosecutor was trying to give all of us life sentences and my attorney was telling me the same. I had no choice but to trust in God, I knew what I had done and now I was being told the possible consequences.

I started ministering to my codefendant, telling him about God, telling him we needed to trust God. He wasn't all that receptive to my words, he was having a hard time in the pod, fearful of the men. Then in the midst of this, I got transferred to the seventh floor, Maximum Security. I prayed for a Christian roommate who could help me continue to grow. And God did that for me again.

My new roommate and I built our lives around reading the Bible, the Word of God, and as I was reading, praying and studying, my demeanor changed. I became more humble and by the grace of God, my mind and heart transformed. My second codefendant, the one I had ministered to previously, then gets put on the same floor as us, mind you we were supposed to be separated, but God had other plans. I started ministering to him again, telling him about God and Jesus and he says, "Yeah, my grandmother has been telling me the same thing." So in the next days we had a Bible study.

Pretty soon the Bible study evolved to having church every day right there on the seventh floor of the jail and before I knew it, a little revival broke out. People were getting saved every day, I'm talking Racketeering RICO cases, murder charges, we saw them all. Often, we looked at the news on TV and we'd see their whole case the night before they entered the pod. All the high-profile cases, big ones, were coming to our floor. I had such a zeal for the Word that anyone who came in was going to hear the Gospel. That is what God did for me. This went on for about two and a half years and I was going in and out of court the whole time, my case was moving forward. But I was a different person than the one at the time of arrest, I had surrendered my life, my selfishness and my pride to have a relationship with Christ. Christ was living through me.

I began to see God move in the lives of others. Our church group prayed for people on the outside, such as a family member struggling with cancer and we saw a healing. We began to see miracles every day, changes in peoples charges, appeals being granted, life sentences being overturned, one of my roommates came off of death row, it was amazing what God was doing.

At the end of two and a half years in the County Jail, I was scheduled for a court appearance and I didn't know what to expect. God was with me. The court dropped my charges from first degree premeditated murder to manslaughter. My life sentence possibility was taken away and was that ever a blessing. I was still praying, telling God that I didn't want to go to prison but at the same time I told Him it was His will, not mine be done. I prayed the same prayer as Jesus prayed in the garden of Gethsemane the night before he was crucified and died.

In 2008 I was sentenced to fifteen years in prison. My first camp was South Florida Reception Center in Miami. When I first got there, I have to admit, I was angry at God. I felt like I was serving Him by preaching. I told God, look this happened and that happened and it's not that I chose to do it, it is that you God, allowed it, you allowed those things to happen. I honestly felt I should have been freed. But I wasn't ready for freedom as is obvious by my thoughts. Many times in our lives we want to be free physically but God still has internal work to do, He works on us until we are ready and when our time comes, only then will we be released.

When I went to prison I started going through a lot of what would end up being different times of growth designed to humble me. I wanted to minister and God told me, "No, allow me to minister through you." During the course of time I learned how to rely on that idea, how to rest in Him and let Him use me. I told God that I wanted to be used as a living sacrifice.

By His grace, I saw Jesus save hundreds of souls in prison. I saw men healed, transformed and delivered to where they had better relationships with their families. I saw men who had lost contact with their families reestablish relationships, they started talking with loved ones where before there was silence. After their encounter with Jesus they were able to call people and communicate better. Family visits increased for these men, which is a big thing to a prisoner. Mail and commissary money started to come to them and those small changes made a lot of difference in their lives and in their hearts. God was having His way.

I served eight years in South Florida Reception Center doing this kind of work and then was transferred to DeSoto Correctional where I spent two years in the annex before I was sent to a work camp. While I was there I saw churches bring new programs, new ministries in for the guys. The atmosphere turned into something beautiful because again, God was moving in the work camp.

All the time I was inside, I was writing little verses of song for God and I shared them with some of the guys and they were like, "Man, these are really good." The prison had talent shows and the guys were telling me that I had to go rap for God, represent God and the Kingdom. I didn't want to do it, I was fearful, but the guys were encouraging me, they told me I had to be able to do it for the Kingdom and to push aside the dark agenda that was prevalent in most of the music out there. They said people needed the light and the life of Christ given to them. Finally they convinced me.

I did the rap for the first time and after I finished I had a guy come up to me who said, "Man, you were rapping, I got goosebumps man, there's something special about what you're doing," and I was surprised when he said that he was being touched by God through the music. When he said that, I realized something entirely different, something new was happening and after praying, God had a talk with me. He let me know that it was through rap that He wanted to touch this generation. I wrote more poetry and music and started doing the music for the guys and I saw hundreds of guys, especially the younger generation get touched by the music.

I got transferred to another prison, Everglades Reentry, and I had the chance to minister through music there too. I joined up with a man who did the sound, Brother Knight. After one of our sessions, a guy came up to me and said, "Hey man, that song you sang on Friday has been going through my head over, over and over - and I gave my life to Christ." When he said that I knew the songs were much more than just the music, God had anointed us, we were bold and stepping out and He had put His hand on us to bring souls to the Kingdom.

I was released in 2019 after being incarcerated for thirteen years. I asked God what He wanted me to do and He asked me back what had I been doing? He said, "Continue."

My birthday is October 24th, it was my first birthday out and I invested in a record label. I knew God called me to do this work, I had seen the fruit of the labor inside, but oddly, I was the type of guy who wanted to just be alone with God, I felt I didn't have the gifts needed or I wasn't even sure I wanted the gifts. I was hesitant. You could say I didn't have confidence to get started.

With God's help and sustenance, I started making songs in obedience and He opened doors, He moved the music forward through His grace. People got in touch with me because the music was both Gospel rap and Gospel reggae and it became popular. Churches and different outreach programs started using the songs to save souls, people were being touched.

Today I have my own clothing line, "DevineTheBrand." I also am part of Urban Youth Justice, UYJ, ministry. We go inside youth prisons where kids from fourteen to eighteen are incarcerated behind razor wire, bars and solid walls, some with multiple charges, some really violent and they have been forgotten. Music is one of the tools we use to disciple and minister to them, they grasp the music. They are really hungry for God and want to listen to the Word and we bring it to them.

In ending, to everyone reading this, be bold about accomplishing the gift God has deposited in you. He has given us all a separate gift, a talent and it makes no difference whether you are in prison or walking the streets, use the gift to the fullest of your ability. Surrender to God your heart, your mind and allow your vessel to be used for His Kingdom purpose. If you are in prison, God can use you as He has used me. Get to the point where you love God with all your heart, mind, soul and strength. I love people around me no matter what they have done because that love can change people, it can change situations, atmospheres. Allow God's love to flow from your heart to theirs.

Aquil Phillip spreads his message through both word and deed, his gifts of poetry and Christian Rap are being used to save lost souls. He is a caring man, a true servant, one who considers other's lives in this world before he considers his own. I have been privileged to witness his ministry in a boys prison, the effectiveness of his message and the impact of his altar call. Like Moses who was at first hesitant to carry God's message, Aquil has been emboldened by the indwelling of the Holy Spirit which carries him forward daily to win souls for God's Kingdom. Below is one of Aquil's songs. Enjoy.

"Stepping Bold"

Stepping in that spirit bold
Taking what the devil stole
Laying hands on the oppressed
In the name of JESUS let' em go
Heal the sick feed the po
Raise the dead free their soul
But not by might or by power but by my spirit says the LORD

Verse :

As I walk thru alley the shadow darkness
I know where his heart is
Holy Spirit going the hardest
Then we laying hands they seeing light
The deaf can hear the blind get sight
We going in to overdrive they know that it is CHRIST ALIVE
We will leave a demon steaming like Stanley
Grab em throw em in the air like a Grammy
We comin thru like it's hurricane sandy
N we here to give u Moore not Mandy

Addendum

Bruce Paulus, National Deputy Director, Damascus Re Entry

Chapter 1
"A Twice Decorated Soldier, A Red Cadillac, And The Death Penalty"
Holland Ricky White

"I told God, "No, this has gone too far!" and I got down on my hands and knees and cried like a baby. The floodgates opened up and <u>I said, "Lord, I'm tired." I surrendered, I completely surrendered.</u> I said to the Lord, "If you allow me an opportunity, I will serve you for the remaining years of my life."

Proverbs 3:5-6 NIV "Trust in the Lord with all your heart and lean not on your own understanding; in all your ways submit to him, and he will make your paths straight.

1. What does it mean to you to "trust in the Lord with all your heart," and how can this level of trust influence decision-making in both personal and professional aspects of life?
2. How can acknowledging God in all our ways impact the direction of our lives, and what practical steps can individuals take to incorporate this principle into their daily routines?
3. In your experience, what are some challenges people face when trying to lean on their own understanding, and how can overcoming those challenges lead to greater spiritual growth and insight?

Chapter 2
"Molestation, Madness and Murder"
Marianne Van Dongen

"There were different instances in the county jail where God spoke clearly and plainly to me through other people. There is no other explanation but God. The first time happened when a woman stood up in a county jail church service and asked, "Who is Marianne?" I was the only Marianne there and she said, <u>"God said for me to tell you</u>

to hold on, that He is here with you, He has not forgotten you and He hears your prayers."

Psalms 34:17 ESV "When the righteous cry for help, the Lord hears and delivers them out of all their troubles"

1. What does it mean to you when the verse states that "the righteous cry out, and the Lord hears them"? How does this shape your understanding of prayer and divine response in times of trouble?
2. In what ways have you experienced or observed God's deliverance in difficult situations, and how does this influence your faith and trust in God's timing and methods of intervention?
3. How can we support and encourage others who may be feeling distressed or oppressed, based on the assurance found in Psalm 34:17 that God is attentive to their cries?

Chapter 3
"Stay Away from That Kid!"
Timothy Kane

"When I got to John's Gospel, I realized that when Jesus was about to go to the cross, He didn't belong there, I belonged there, and that's when something changed in me; I perceived that He was willing to lay down his life for me. I was guilty, yet He was willing to go to the cross for me.

He took my place. Since that day, September 12, 1993, when I discovered all of this, I would never be the same. His resurrection made sense to me. I lit up with joy knowing I had an eternal life with Him. My heart was free. I had never known real freedom before this, I was learning about bondage daily but I knew that even if my life was taken, it's a drop in the bucket compared to eternity. Because of what Jesus had given me, I knew that if I had to spend the rest of my life in prison, and I say this even now after spending twenty-five years of my life behind bars, if I had to do another twenty or even fifty, Jesus was worth it…"

"God made him who had no sin to be sin for us, so that in him we might become the righteousness of God" (2 Corinthians 5:21)

1. What does it mean to you personally to have someone who was sinless take on your sins, and how does this concept influence your understanding of grace and forgiveness?
2. In what ways do you believe that becoming the "righteousness of God" through faith impacts how we live our daily lives and interaction with others?
3. How can understanding the sacrifice made on our behalf challenge or change our perceptions of our own worth and identity in Christ?

Chapter 4
"Darwin, I Did This for You"
Casey Diaz

"When she left that day, Francis Proctor began prayer intercession for a year and a half over my life. I really believe that it was her prayer and her obedience to her call to pray for me that brought me to a point where I had an encounter with Christ in my cell…."

James 5:13-16 ESV "Is anyone among you suffering? Let him pray. Is anyone cheerful? Let him sing praise. Is anyone among you sick? Let him call for the elders of the church, and let them pray over him, anointing him with oil in the name of the Lord. And the prayer of faith will save the one who is sick, and the Lord will raise him up. And if he has committed sins, he will be forgiven. Therefore, confess your sins to one another and pray for one another, that you may be healed. The prayer of a righteous person has great power as it is working."

1. How do you interpret the relationship between prayer and healing as described in this passage, and what implications does it have for your own approach to prayer in times of trouble or illness?
2. In what ways can confessing our sins to one another, as mentioned in these verses, strengthen our relationships within a community of faith and promote spiritual growth?
3. What insights do you gain from the idea that the prayer of a righteous person is powerful and effective, and how does this shape your understanding of the role of faith in overcoming challenges?

Chapter 5
"Drugs: The Devil's Communion"
Brandon Boyce

"While I was in the jail awaiting trial, in my mind I kept hearing songs that were sung in Westgate Tabernacle Church. They flooded my mind, the words kept coming back to me. Songs like, "Open the Eyes of My Heart," and a song by Casting Crowns, "East to West." The song talked about our sins being cast by God as far as the East is from the West. They were the songs that I had sung, and God was using the words to draw me back to Him."

Colossians 3:16 ESV "Let the word of Christ dwell in you richly, teaching and admonishing one another in all wisdom, singing psalms and hymns and spiritual songs, with thankfulness in your hearts to God."

1. How can we practically let the word of Christ dwell in us richly in our daily lives, and what impact do you think this has on our interactions with others within the faith community?
2. In what ways do you believe in teaching and admonishing one another through music and spiritual songs? How can Christian song lyrics foster deeper relationships among believers, and how can this practice be enhanced in your church or community?
3. What does it mean to you personally to sing with gratitude in your hearts to God, and how might this expression of worship influence your emotional and spiritual well-being?

Chapter 6
"Don't Play with God"
Adam Jolly

"So, I wasn't too afraid when I was put into a one-man cell at the Juvenile Detention Center. To my surprise, church services were offered, so I attended. I heard some familiar words and people I didn't know prayed with me. Living with Ma Jennie, as strange as it sounds, church was mandatory for all us kids. She tried to teach us a reverence for God and to develop a respect for His word, but we weren't willing to surrender our rebellious ways. Jesus was a Sunday kind of thing. I can still hear her prayers today: "Lord, don't let the Devil kill my boys."

Proverbs 9:10 NASB "The fear of the LORD is the beginning of wisdom, And the knowledge of the Holy One *is* understanding.

1. How do you understand the concept of the "fear of the Lord" as described in this verse, and how this understanding might shape one's approach to wisdom and knowledge in everyday life?
2. In your experience, what are some practical ways that individuals can demonstrate reverence for God, and how do these actions contribute to a deeper understanding of wisdom?
3. What role do you believe humility plays in the pursuit of knowledge, and how can recognizing our limitations enhance our ability to learn and grow spiritually?

Chapter 7
"Monster Man and an Angel's Face"
Alonzo Dixon

My grandparents instilled Jesus in me at a young age, they planted the seed. They were always preaching Jesus. They were married seventy years. When I was around them, I was in church or I was required to read the Bible. I knew about God and Jesus because of the influence they had on me. When I was with my grandparents it was either Sunday School or the belt so the easy decision was Sunday School. But all that teaching, all that time they put into me, went out the window when I went home to my mother, the alcoholism and drug addiction that was part of her life.

Proverbs 22:6 NASB "Train up a child in the way he should go, even when he grows older, he will not abandon it."

1. What do you think are the key components of "training up a child in the way he should go," and how can parents and caregivers effectively implement these components in today's diverse cultural context?
2. In what ways can the principles outlined in Proverbs 22:6 apply not only to parenting but also to mentoring or guiding people of all ages, and how might this impact community relationships?

3. How do you interpret the idea that "when he is old, he will not depart from it," and what implications does this have for understanding the long-term effects of early teachings and values instilled in children?

Chapter 8
"A Scream and Then…"
Aquil Phillip

"It's interesting how God will put certain people in your life and maybe plant a seed that we don't even pay attention to. But years later, that comes back."

1 Corinthians 3:6-9, NLT, "I planted the seed in your hearts, and Apollos watered it, but it was God who made it grow." It's not important who does the planting, or who does the watering. What's important is that God makes the seed grow. The one who plants and the one who waters work together for the same purpose and both will be rewarded for their own hard work. For both are God's workers.

1. What does Paul mean when he emphasizes that it is God who gives the growth, and how does this perspective influence our understanding of success and the effectiveness of our efforts in personal endeavors?
2. How do you interpret the metaphor of being 'co-workers' with God, and what responsibilities and roles do you think this entails for believers in their communities?
3. In what ways can recognizing that we are all part of God's larger work help us appreciate the contributions of others in our spiritual journeys, regardless of their roles or status?

AUTHOR BIO

Ken attended the University of Southern California, BA, Zoology, and St. Catherine's College, Cambridge University England, as a Cambridge Scholar in 1964. He was commissioned as an Officer, US Army, 1966. Volunteering for Airborne and Special Forces training, he graduated from Jump Master and US Army John F. Kennedy Center for Special Warfare School in 1967.

Ken served in the US Army 3rd Special Forces Group, the 5th Special Forces Group and the 25th Division, Vietnam. He was decorated with a Silver Star for Gallantry, Bronze Star for Valor, Vietnamese Cross For Gallantry, and Purple Heart for wounds received. After serving in the U.S. Military, Ken joined the Federal Bureau of Investigation as a Special Agent, specializing in bank robbery and fugitive investigations in Philadelphia, Washington Field Office, and Los Angeles. After the FBI, he started Surfside Development Company, a real estate development firm that he currently owns and manages. Married with one son and now living in Florida, he is involved with various charitable projects sponsored by Lean On Me USA.

As CEO of Lean On Me USA, he is the producer of the Death or Prison podcast, bringing faith, hope, God Almighty and His Son Jesus Christ into homes and prisons through GloryStar Satellite Television, Roku TV and more than 1,500,000 electronic tablets distributed in prisons nationwide.

www.ingramcontent.com/pod-product-compliance
Lightning Source LLC
Chambersburg PA
CBHW062108080426
42734CB00012B/2793